Migration and Family:

Secrets to Sustainability for Culturally Diverse Families

Ephraim Osaghae MBA, MBL, PMP

ISBN 978-0-6453744-0-7

DEDICATION

I dedicate this book to all families and everyone

that care about families.

Family is worth it!

ACKNOWLEDGMENT

I want to thank my family. You provide me with the space, love, and experience that motivate me to seek, find, and treasure balance.

I also want to acknowledge friends, colleagues, and neighbours along my life journey to date. I am blessed to be part of a viable community.

My story is incomplete without you.

Table of Contents

Chapter 1

Introduction

Musa (not the real name) arrived in Australia on a student visa to pursue a post-graduate qualification. Like many students from less developed countries, he planned to remain permanently in Australia after studying. But unfortunately, he couldn't find a suitable job after graduation. This situation put him under immense pressure because securing a visa to stay permanently in the country depends on demonstrating the capacity to be employed in a relevant field of study. So, Musa got desperate and explored an alternative visa pathway. He met a citizen, Jenna (not the real name), who could sponsor his visa application while building a family together. As a result, Musa and Jenna commenced a de facto relationship – they lived together without being legally married. Australia formally recognises de facto relationships. Such couples are entitled to virtually every benefit, just like their married counterparts. They can receive child benefits, tax benefits, first home buyers grants, sponsorships for Partner visas, etc.

Unfortunately, Jenna was addicted to alcohol and often abusive towards him. Musa felt he'd had enough and tried to confront her. But Jenna threatened to withdraw her sponsorship of his visa if Musa did not remain *accommodating*. Musa did try to take things as they are for a while, but he comes from a cultural background where men are not as compliant. They got into a domestic argument which increasingly became uncontrollable. True to her threats, Jenna withdrew her sponsorship despite pleas from close friends of the couple. Sadly, Musa was eventually deported to Africa to start life over again.

John (not the real name) moved to Canada as a skilled immigrant to advance his Data Analytics career and raise his family in a place of high living standards. John has a high-paying job that helped him invite Jane (not the real name), his wife, and his children. Everything was perfect until the couple had a profound misunderstanding. So, John decided to travel home to his extended family back in Kenya, Africa. John's mother introduced another woman to him, and he stayed around for a while to start a family with her. On getting back to Canada, Jane was happy to have her husband back, unaware of all that had happened during John's trip. She thought they'd live happily ever after.

Soon, she found out about the other woman. The family never remain the same after that. There was so much pain, anger, and distrust. Unfortunately for Jane, she has detached from most of her friends and families back in Kenya who could have stepped into the matter and culturally resolved the issue. She also lacked a network of trusted friends in Canada. She is still dependent on John regarding her legal status in Canada. Jane's mental health deteriorated due to the chronic feeling of helplessness and isolation. Worse still, their cultural background has shaped them into the type of people that do not believe in therapy.

The impact extended to the children, and they were beginning to struggle with schoolwork and friendship. Though the Kenyan community in Canada knew that all was not too well with the family, they couldn't do much about it because privacy and maintaining personal spaces were challenging boundaries to break when supporting community members regarding family issues.

You see, visa approval to migrate with family is happy news for many. *The land is always greener across the hill*. From the desire for a more robust economy to accessing better living standards and the pride of living abroad, migration often holds exciting opportunities. Indeed, there're many proofs and lived experiences to validate the benefits of migration.[1]

However, after the *honeymoon phase* of moving abroad, reality often pushes people, especially families, to disturbing extremes. The change frequently strains their mental resources and relationship, dash their expectations, and threaten their stability. Globally, immigrants often face difficulties accessing health care, housing, education, employment, etc. In addition, they may become easy targets for abuse, extortion, and exploitation due to lack of a protective family network, lack of information, or gaps in immigration status.[2] Language barriers, access to local services, cultural differences, raising children, and prejudice[3] are just a few of the challenges that many families would have to confront without much help or insight.

All the while, immigration and family issues have craved our attention for so long. But, so long, we've turned blind eyes and deaf ears, worrying about what side we're on rather than working together to fix the problems. And when anyone tries to speak up, they are often criticised or even discredited.

---

[1] A Handbook for Migrants: The Good, The Challenges and The Lessons, Tri-W Pty Ltd 2019
[2] https://www.icrc.org/en/document/speech-migration-and-internal-displacement-national-and-global-challenges
[3] https://www.immigroup.com/topics/top-10-problems-immigrants/

Yet, issues don't just go away. Someone often must *take the risk to shine some light on the matter*. Being that person could leave you feeling vulnerable: you don't know what to expect, but you're moving toward a goal that's worth the risk. That's what writing this book means to the author: it's a risky venture for various reasons.

Firstly, the "sacredness" of the family unit makes it a delicate subject even in contemporary times. There is always that question of whether one is knowledgeable enough to write on such a complex, and often, no-one-size-fit-all matter. "What if I say something about family that's deeply offensive, rightly or wrongly?"

Secondly, privacy is associated with the family context. People can chat about many aspects of their lives but family. It is commonly considered a very personal matter. "What if more people walk past this book just because it addresses a subject they don't want to confront and would prefer to keep private?"

Thirdly, few things in life go deep, broad, and lasting as family issues. Family issues often require advanced knowledge and expertise to unpack and resolve; sometimes, it requires clinical therapy. "What if someone thinks the author is not qualified to talk about family?"

Also, writing about family as a male author may make some people want to read the book, while others may think that the views would be biased. To extend this point a bit more, what if the male author resides in the western world, in an era when women's rights are the heightened focus across all sectors? A clime where gender equality is the norm is a right foot on the right track. Arguably, a male writer can address family without the fear of "writing to offend" in such dispensation. Of course, readers may need to cut the author some slack; a man will always be a man no matter how he tries to be politically and socially correct.

Some male authors who write on the family's subject have their upbringing in cultures where gender equality campaign has not taken centre stage. This situation could further amplify the dilemma. Indeed, immigrants from such cultures must learn to adopt and adapt fast for the good of all stakeholders—especially the family. The author of this book can only hope the impact is worth the read. This book offers vital considerations for sustainability in culturally diverse families in the context of global mobility and immigration.

Global mobility is not a new subject; it is almost as old as humanity. People relocate for various reasons. Tourism, study, work, business, family, and protection are the most popular, especially with the significant changes that require more permanent relocation, which is the focus of this book.

Stakeholders do not often consider some factors associated with family immigration as much as they should. There is neither documented nor well-circulated data to enable better planning, better preparations, and better outcomes for all parties. Hopefully, this book can add to sustainable migration and sustainable family experiences.

As you read and reflect on the contents of this book, you'll gain a chance to re-evaluate migration and its impacts on families —the good, the challenges, and critical lessons. It gives much attention to culturally diverse families. It also directs valuable attention towards multicultural and migrant men because of this cohort's unique and urgent requirements. The aim is not to open a gender debate. Much of that is already in the mainstream. Research and lived experiences of the author drive it. Nevertheless, there should be value for everyone with a man in their lives - a son, father, husband, brother, nephew, cousin, colleague, partner, neighbour, and friend.

Ultimately, this book draws vital links between immigration, multicultural families, and overall community wellbeing. It also provides some future projections. The author makes a case for preserving and promoting the worth of the family unit. Are you ready to explore?

1.1 Let's define some keywords in the context of this book
Family

The Family has become a complex narrative in contemporary times. But let's adopt the definition in the Oxford English Dictionary for simplicity and relevance: [4] *A family is a group of people, traditionally consisting of parents and their children, living together as a household (at least for a reasonable period until the children leave to raise a branch of the family tree, conventionally)*. In this context, blood, marriage, adoption, etc., connect family members. They would have long-term commitments to each other.

Immigration

This is the action of *immigrating*, i.e., entering a country to settle there. This mobility is a global occurrence. However, the Australian context is the main case study and reference for

---

[4] Oxford English Dictionary, Oxford University Press, London 2021

this book. Thus, an Australian migrant is a person who was born overseas whose usual residence (12 months or more) is in Australia.[5] About 30% of the 25 million people living in Australia were born overseas (immigrants) as of 30 June 2016.[6] Table 1.1 further represents a breakdown of these statistics, which indicates that there are more immigrants in Australia born in England, India, and China in that decreasing order.

Table 1.1: Australia's population by top 10 countries of birth

Country of birth(a)	'000	%(b)
England	980	3.8
India	721	2.8
China	651	2.5
New Zealand	565	2.2
Philippines	310	1.2
Vietnam	270	1.1
South Africa	200	0.8
Italy	178	0.7
Malaysia	177	0.7
Sri Lanka	147	0.6
All overseas-born	7,654	29.8
Australian-born	18,043	70.2

a. **Top 10 countries of birth for overseas-born as of 30 June 2020.**
b. **Proportion of the total population of Australia.**

---

[5] Glossary of ABS Report 3415.0 - Migrant Data Matrices, 2012 (http://www.abs.gov.au),)
[6] Migration, Australia June 2020, Australian Bureau of Statistics (www.abs.gov.au – accessed 28 September 2021)

Culturally Diverse

Also known as culturally and linguistically diverse (CaLD), this term is a broad term for describing people and communities with diverse languages, ethnic backgrounds, nationalities, traditions, societal structures, and religions. The term has been further qualified in Australia to represent groups and individuals other than Aboriginal or Torres Strait Islander, Anglo Saxon, or Anglo Celtic.[7] Thus, countries like England, Northern Ireland, Scotland, USA, Canada, Ireland, and Wales are excluded from the CaLD narrative as per the latter definition.

The terms culturally diverse, CaLD, and multicultural are often used interchangeably in this book to describe people, families, and communities with various cultural and ethnic backgrounds.

Secrets

If you type secret on Google, you'll have nearly 10 billion results in less than 1 second. This is because it appears there's so much out there about secrets. We use the definition from Cambridge Dictionary, which describes *a secret as a piece of information that one person or only a few people know. Or a*

---

[7] Community Grants Program, Office of Multicultural Interests (OMI) 2020, (www.omi.wa.gov.au – accessed 28 September 2021)

fact about a subject that is not known.[8] The objective of including this term as part of the title is not to judge anyone for their secrets. Instead, it aims to unveil some facts that can enhance sustainability for families in the context of immigration.

Sustainability

Sustainability is a concept that has remained relevant despite how it has become politicized for various reasons. It is defined as the capacity to be upheld or defended as valid, correct, or authentic.[9] Practically, it is doing things today, whether climate, business, or, in the context of this book, family, in such a way that the future is preserved.

1.2 Purpose of this Book

This book does not blame all the challenges associated with culturally diverse families on immigration. Non-immigrant also experience difficulties. Moreover, some immigrant and multicultural families are live their dreams almost in all aspects of family life.

The author of this book does not boast of having all the answers to all situations, not even the least. Instead, he offers insights based on lived experiences as a CaLD, Nigerian-

---

[8] https://dictionary.cambridge.org/dictionary/english/secret (accessed 28 November 2021)
[9] Oxford English Dictionary, Oxford University Press, London 2021.

Australian, residing in Australia for almost two decades with his family. He has experienced the significant benefits and challenges of immigration and permanent residence in the West. Like his other books in this genre, he aims to provide practical information and guidance that will make it easier for intending, new and not-so-new immigrants and culturally diverse people.

The man in the family, the husband, father, and male partner, has received a sizeable share of attention in this book – for the benefits and sustainability of the whole. However, the lessons can provide some wisdom for all members of the family unit and other stakeholders.

1.3 Audience

Intending immigrants can reflect on key aspects of this book and use it as a guide to plan and prepare for the big move. People do not often consider the complete picture and implications of the relocation process. The focus is usually the excitement of visa approval and preparations for the trip. Intending immigrants have the best opportunities to maximize the gains and minimize the pains associated with immigration and family. Few changes and shifts in mindsets at the front-end can help enhance the benefits and avoid costly errors, not just for the primary visa holder but also for the entire family down the track.

New and more settled immigrants, including international students, can also approach this matter like intending migrants, except their case is not about preparations. Instead, it is about taking the next decisive steps to ensure success regarding family life aspirations. There is still time to make necessary adjustments that will set them on the path for achieving their goals while ensuring sustainability in the critical aspect of family, even if they are yet to start one.

This book will also provide valuable insights to policymakers and ministerial delegates, especially those involved in immigration matters. It is indisputable that stability in the family unit provides the pillar and stability for the wider community. Offering opportunities for people to immigrate into one's country can go a long way to helping families, including providing them freedom from war, resettlement, employment, business opportunities, etc.

However, there are also numerous cases where this has caused significant challenges to family life. Just emphasising the point again, this is not about apportioning blames on the host governments and policymakers. Instead, this book provides additional references and information to consider regarding immigration for the sustainability of the family unit, especially for culturally diverse members of our community.

Residents, students, and professionals can read, reflect, and develop the necessary cultural intelligence, which has become increasingly high demand considering the cultural diversity in our neighbourhoods, schools, and workplaces. The content of this book will also provide researchers with additional references and ideas for relevant studies.

This book contains vital points for considerations, for lasting solutions, lasting outcomes, and across a broad spectrum of audiences. While Australia is the main case study, the principles apply to many other contexts and countries involving immigration and culturally diverse families. It is about life and community, and we are all in it together.

Chapter 2

Immigration and CaLD Families: Is It Really Worth It?

Different intentions and goals drive people to take the remarkable leap of faith in relocating to a new country and start all over again. It ranges from the more voluntary drivers of business and skilled migration to the less-voluntary humanitarian migration of fleeing war situations, seeking asylum, etc.

Is it worth it? Is it worth it from the family context? Are families better off because of immigration? Do we take the time and effort to check our key success criteria? Do we acknowledge and celebrate successes and progress made? Does it get better with time and with generations? Are goals and aspirations realized? Even in situations where set goals are achieved, does success come at a cost? Are there opportunity costs that are forfeited? The answers to these questions would significantly depend on individual contexts, of course; there is no 'one answer fits all' situation, and this book does not suggest having that at all.

However, there are some common trends worth highlighting. A balanced view is necessary for such a potentially provocative question (or sets of questions). The author presented such perspectives in his previous books including insights from his lived experiences and insights from engaging with culturally diverse people as a community leader and executive of a not-for-profit organization.[10] [11] [12] Indeed, the matter deserves exploring *the good, the challenges, and the lessons.*

2.1 The Good

Typically, when the motivations for the big move are being considered, people focus more on the good and beneficial aspects rather than the challenges they would likely have to confront at a later period after arrival in the new country of residence. For some, they are in flight mode, understandably. They just want to get out of their 'pain points at that time. Indeed, the good aspects of relocating to the west are more visible irrespective of the pathways of

---

[10] A Handbook for Migrants: The Good, The Challenges and The Lessons, Tri-W Pty Ltd 2019

[11] Voices from Home: Wisdom from Our Diasporic Roots, Tri-W Pty Ltd 2019

[12] Adopt Adapt Achieve: An Amazing Triple A Guide for Successful Relocation, Change and Integration, Tri-W Pty Ltd 2020

immigration, i.e., studying, work, business, family, or humanitarian visas. See Figure 2.1 for a simplified illustration of the motivations for a family relocation.

Figure 2.1: Illustration of motivations for family relocation

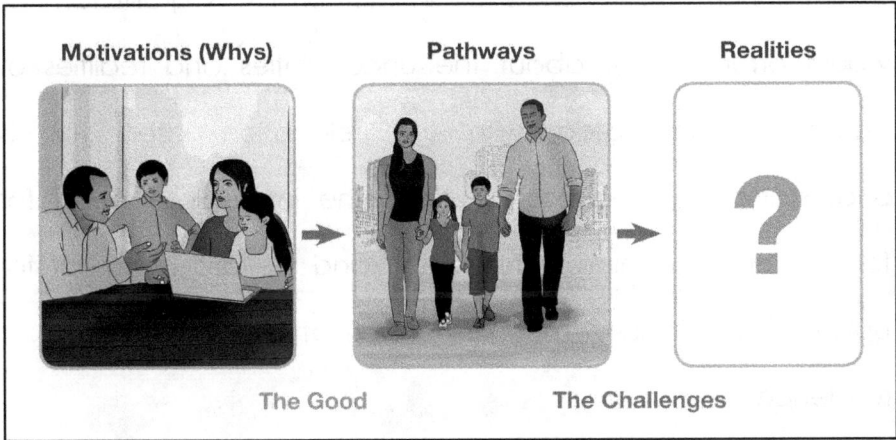

Indeed, there are beneficial aspects of immigration to the western world especially in the family. Economic prosperity, a better life for the family, and a higher standard of living conditions are three commonly cited value drivers.

2.1.1 Economic prosperity

Generally, economic stability is a critical determining factor for people wanting to relocate to the West. The relative availability and access to economic opportunities are vital driving forces for embarking on such a journey. Research and reality have shown that some cities in the West are economically richer than whole countries in some parts of the world's less developed regions. This situation has continued to trigger the motivation and action of relocating from the latter to take up permanent residence in the former. Migrant families would often bother about the uncertainties and realities of challenges associated with the relocation later. This is understandable because typically, the immediate need for food, shelter, clothing, safety, etc., and welfare payment for upkeep, are largely met on arrival at the new place of residence.

2.1.2 Better Life for Family

A better life for the entire family often takes centre stage when CaLD families deliberate on the purpose of relocating to the West. Some attractive features include better security, education, health, real options, and economic opportunities for a secured future. Indeed, the results of comparing life outcomes of children who relocated versus those of their contemporaries who grew up and remained in their country of origin often justify why the future of children continues to feature as a significant reason for immigration to the West. See Figure 2.2 for a simplified illustration of this reality. Children that could have been hindered by unfortunate situations of hunger, wars, sub-standard education, security concerns, etc., can now seize the opportunities of an economically viable and safe environment to grow and be the best they can be. Again, families will relegate considerations of the associated uncertainties to the future.

Figure 2.2: Illustration of motivations for family relocation (Children and Youth)

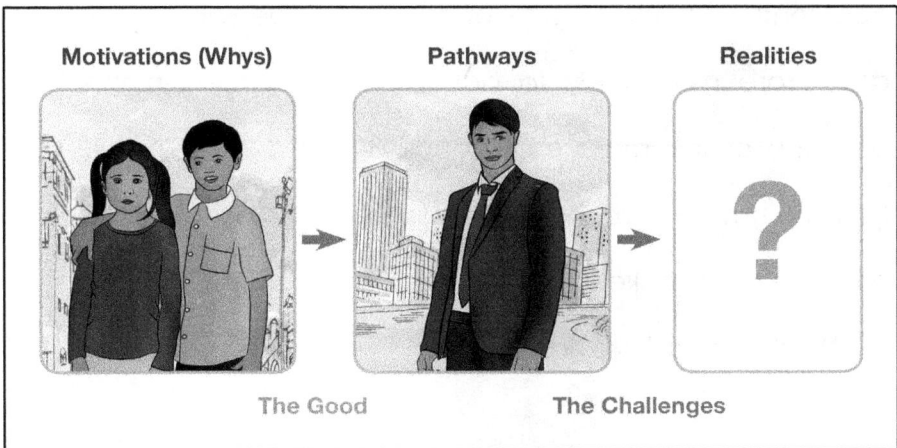

2.1.3 Higher Standard of Living Conditions

The desire for a better standard of living is another big pull to the option of migrating. Living in most parts of the West presents this lifestyle unmistakably. Let's consider a few of them, which the author can confirm, especially from lived experiences in Australia.

There are excellent road networks with world-class planned and actual maintenance, and ongoing management. It is not surprising that the rate of traffic-related deaths is less in western countries (see Figure 2.3).[13] [14] Of course, there are other contributory factors to the cause of road accidents including road rules, car mechanic status, weather conditions, driver status, etc. Nevertheless, a positive correlation between traffic accidents and the quality of roads is undeniable. Moreover, drivers are more likely to adhere to road rules in the West because of the more enforceability of the law. Similarly, cars that are not roadworthy are less likely to get on the road in the West. One is less likely to die from road accidents while living in the West. This fact provides another incentive for relocation.

[13] WHO, ed. (2015). "WHO Report 2015: Data tables" (official report). World Health Organization, Geneva.
[14] WHO, ed. (2018). Global Status Report on Road Safety 2018 (official report). World Health Organization, Geneva. pp. xiv–xv, 1–13

Figure 2.3: List of countries by traffic-related death rate

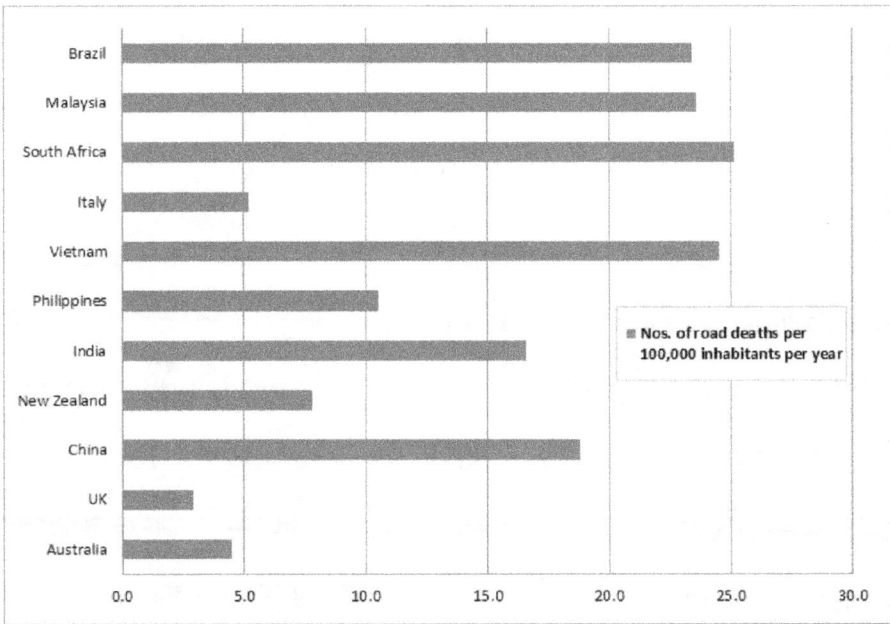

Note: 10 countries shown – like Table 1.1. with Brazil added for South America representation

The utilities are often seamlessly regular. Water, gas, and electricity were constant for weeks and months without disruptions. The need for standby generators is almost non-existent. Communities have experienced those once-in-a-year types of disruptions over the years in Australia, as an example, due to situations like significant storm events, planned maintenance, etc. However, on such occasions, there are usually several announcements via various mass media providing advance notices or explanations for the disruption and information on measures to avoid harm to people and properties. Likewise, the organised refuse collection system is remarkable, including separate bins for recyclable and non-recyclable wastes. The duty of care and accountability are unmissable. And that has not changed over time.

Furthermore, the organisation and ease of access to medical services were aspects of living in a country like Australia that has made immigrants feel so blessed to migrate to the country. Typically, you or any member of your family would be able to see a medical doctor situated close to your place of residence within a short timeframe of requesting an appointment. All you need is usually evidence that you are an Australian permanent resident. Another exciting thing is that the services are bulk billed (i.e., you did not have to pay anything). Prescribed sets of medication were highly subsidized as well.

The law also works in most western countries, at least in relative terms. No one is above the law. Over the years, we have seen cases where people high-up in government have been brought to justice for crimes such as traffic infringements, unapproved spending of government funds, etc. There is no pleading for pardon when caught on the *wrong side of the law.* Any attempt to bribe or argue your way out of the offence will only attract heavier penalties. The police have brutally taken on gangs and many situations that caused fear and panic within neighbourhoods, but they usually brought things to order promptly almost all the time. Unlike many other regions in the world where the 'common man' feels visibly hopeless and emasculated to voice out issues of concern even when there is so much injustice.

To cap it up, there is a feeling of safety and security as you go about life's duties each day. Generally, you do not need to be dubious to afford a reasonably good life. The system is relatively equitable in terms of the law. It is not surprising that life expectancy has been consistently higher for people living in western countries (see Table 2.1).

Table 2.1: Life expectancy at birth, top 10 countries in the world

Country	Persons(a)	Male	Female
Japan	84.47 (rank 1)	81.33 (rank 4)	87.51 (rank 1)
Switzerland	83.63 (rank 2)	81.69 (rank 1)	85.47 (rank 5)
Singapore	83.46 (rank 3)	81.34 (rank 2)	85.58 (rank 4)
Spain	83.43 (rank 4)	80.69 (rank 10)	86.12 (rank 2)
Italy	83.35 (rank 5)	81.13 (rank 7)	85.41 (rank 7)
Australia	83.28 (rank 6)	81.31 (rank 5)	85.27 (rank 8)
Channel Islands	82.93 (rank 7)	80.97 (rank 8)	84.8 (rank 9)
Iceland	82.86 (rank 8)	81.34 (rank 2)	84.37 (rank 15)
Republic of Korea	82.85 (rank 9)	79.72 (rank 18)	85.79 (rank 3)
Israel	82.82 (rank 10)	81.14 (rank 6)	85.79 (rank 3)

a. **Based on life expectancy for persons (citing UN's World Population Prospects 2019, Rev. 1 as primary source)**

These factors contribute to a higher standard of living in the West with significant motivation for migration, even singly. Imagine the impact when they present as a combined set of incentives! However, there is another side of the coin despite all efforts to overlook what that could mean for the sustainability of families. Wisdom demands a holistic approach to things, especially as significant as immigration.

2.2 The Challenges

Despite the 'greener pasture' associated with immigration as described in the previous section, there are also challenges. Intending immigrants hardly think about the challenging aspects, especially when there is so much excitement about relocating from less developed countries to the usually more developed western world. "What can be worse than my current situation?" they would conclude. However, it does not take that long for the realities on the ground to become evident while settling into the new places of residence. We use the classical theory of Abraham Maslow's hierarchy of needs to explain these typically time-based experiences (see Figure 2.4).

Figure 2.4: Illustration of the dynamics between the benefits (good) and challenges of family Relocation

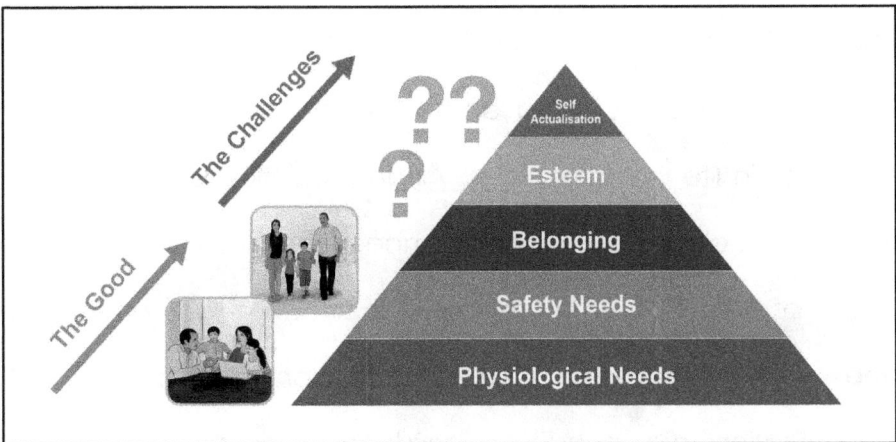

The benefits of meeting physiological and safety needs (e.g., clean and adequate water, food, clothing, and shelter) are evident upon relocating to the West. The welfare system in Australia, for example, would ensure that people will have these needs met even if they cannot financially afford them. The same situation applies to the needs of accessible health care, security, and safety. However, they would begin to experience the challenges regarding higher-level needs after settling into the system. For example, they may not meet their need for a sense of belonging (friendship, connections, economic participation, etc.). The gaps are also evident with the requirement for esteem and self-actualization (living to your fullest potentials).

Consider a case study of a skilled immigrant and his family that seized the opportunity to relocate to Australia from Sri Lanka. They were excited about the immediate and positive changes in life circumstances. All uncertainties relating to their basic physiological and safety needs may quickly become things of the past as they settle into their new country and life in the West. However, the need for belonging, esteem, self-actualization did constitute challenges for the family and individual members. The male partner and father of two children has a graduate degree in Mechanical Engineering and significant work experience. He yearned for an opportunity to use his qualification and skills. He would have preferred to stop his current 'survival' job and commence a role as an Engineer and grow a career of his aspirations. The situation is the same with his spouse, a qualified nurse. She would have preferred to use her skills at some earlier point in time rather than caring for the children full time. The void created by the higher needs of belonging, esteem, self-actualisation became increasingly visible. They could not fill it despite their efforts. The scope of this book does not cover reasons for these employment issues and how to bridge the gaps. See other books by the author for more perspectives on these equally essential aspects of valuing and maximising the benefits of culturally diverse professionals. [15] [16] [17]

This same pattern is usually applicable to multicultural children and youth (see Figure 2.5). However, the causes of lack of belonging, esteem, and self-actualisation may be different. Like their parents, children relocate to the West with excitement.

---

[15] Adopt Adapt Achieve: An Amazing Triple A Guide for Successful Relocation, Change and Integration
[16] Migrapreneurs: The Potentials for Diversifying our Diversity
[17] Top Insiders Guide to Successful and Stable Careers: How to Secure and Sustain Professional Jobs Without Losing Self and Value

They often value freedom, the variety of fun things to do and places to go, the feeling of more safety, etc. But it does not take much time to observe that these other needs are unmet in many cases. Following periods of keeping within the family, they would need to go to school, play sports, meet up with their mates, etc., outside the 'safety net' of family and familiar home territory. Cases of being segregated as the 'other,' or even outright bullying, are not uncommon. Like adults, children and youth will respond differently to the frustration of not meeting these needs. The level of assurance that children have about their identity would be critically important in navigating such a trying period.

Figure 2.5: Illustration of the dynamics between the benefits and challenges of family Relocation (Children & Youth)

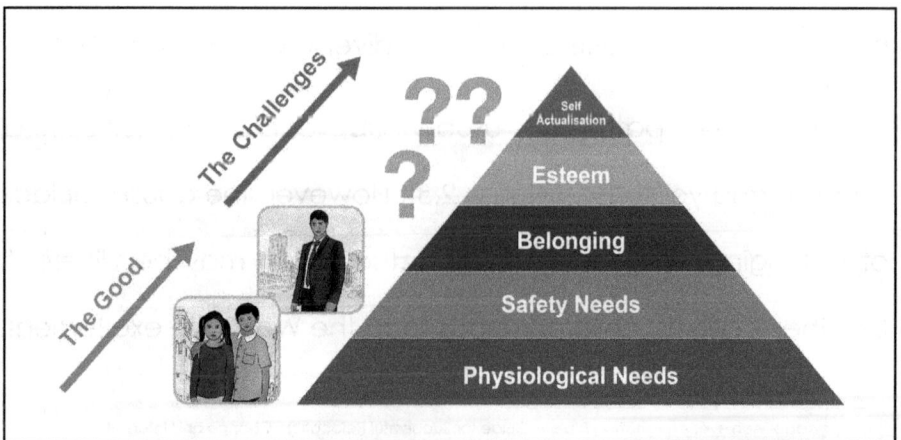

The ripple effects of these unmet needs would potentially be associated with culture shocks and conflicts, maladaptation, the tension in the home and at work, non-functioning family units, separation (at various levels), and physical and mental health problems.

Before we look at these points more closely, it is essential to emphasize that one should not attribute every challenge in culturally diverse families to immigration. Family issues often have root causes traceable to other sources, including personality types, childhood experiences, life experiences, events before marriage, and relocation. It is a complex issue that is typically more than just the impact of immigration. However, the latter is undeniable, and this is the focus of this book. It aims to unpack the realities of these challenges based on research, observations, and lived experiences. It contributes to enhancing the knowledge, processes, and systems for proactively addressing the challenges as reasonably practicable for the sustainability of families.

2.2.1 Culture shocks and conflicts

Moving from a comfort zone with presumed constants requires some courage. The same applies to relocating to an entirely new country and culture, not just for tourism but for permanent residency.

Usually, immigrants do not know what to expect. First, there are limitless uncertainties. Even when they read books, articles, or consulted maps (including the famous Google map) about their destination, there're no guarantees. There're always surprises on arrival.

No doubt, there is usually this bubble of excitement when leaving a place for a *better* one. This relocation often entails leaving behind security threats, poor social amenities, unemployment issues, and low social and economic impact. In this context, the new location (the western world) promises the opposite – a technologically robust economy, more amenities, better employment opportunities, access to social welfare, and more safety and human rights.

However, the initial excitement may fade away, especially when unmet expectations and the reality and demands of change set in. At this point, some immigrants experience weariness, loss, and confusion. Others have recalled feeling regretful and unsure about the following line of action. Thoughts like, "Did I miss it somewhere? I thought I did my homework well," will flood their minds.

Yet, they would have to keep fighting to overcome the shocks associated with such significant shifts during these unpleasant contemplations, including those related to family, work, community, and even weather conditions. These are just a few everyday experiences that add to the pressure and enormous burden, especially during the early phase of settling into a new country. Moreover, the feeling of guilt and failure to meet the financial expectations back in their homelands would only make things worse.

There is also the issue of cultural conflicts and a clash of values. One should particularly empathize with culturally diverse young people because they often get caught in the middle of all the massive changes that are going on around them. They experience a bombardment of information, new cultures, and shifting values. It could become frustrating for them when they try to process and make sense of it, including their sense of identity. Even just practical aspects of what they should do and what they should not do, in certain circumstances, could become a challenge and potential trigger for stress and tension.

Immigrants come into a different culture in the West, where parents and children's relationship dynamics are often dissimilar to their former country or ethnic backgrounds. Usually, parents of CaLD backgrounds often assume that their children (including those born in the new country) should understand the concept and practices of their own cultures of upbringing.

Instead, the children (from CaLD backgrounds) get connected to cultures and norms in the West, in schools, via TV and social media, friendship groups, etc. On top of that, children of CaLD parents often identify with the country they were born instead of their parent's country of birth. This means, for instance, children of Australian migrants would let you know that they are Australians and it's their parents that came from Country X.

Most migrant parents don't have any trouble with their children identifying with their western country of birth in this context. They want it, some with passionate intentionality. However, many parents are rarely ready to see their children dissociate from the parent's nationality, culture, values, and even family tree.

Are the children responsible for the 'cultural gaps?' No! The cultures of their CaLD parents are often new to them. Why should they be expected to embrace such *foreign cultures*? Even with CaLD children who immigrated with their parents, it doesn't take much time to acculturate to western cultures.

Integrating into a new culture without adequate preparation by both parents and their children can be conflicting, stressful, and life changing. Cultural norms and values may need revisiting. For example, a child of CaLD parents may not appreciate the 'expectations' to bow down (or even stand upright) to greet a parent first thing in the morning. They may not also see the value of keeping in touch with grandparents, who are sort of strangers to them. Any attempt to 'force' it could (and did often) result in tension and conflicts in families.

Cultural shocks and conflicts are sensitive because the situation has led to the breakdown of relationships and litigations in some cases. More severe instances have resulted in children being forcibly removed from their family homes and placed in Government-sponsored foster homes, with all the associated implications.

Blending your family into a new culture demands kindness and understanding on all sides: parents should empathize with their children, especially those born in the West. Growing up in western culture is all these children know (despite the efforts of some parents to promote their cultural background and practices in their homes).

For example, CaLD parents who expect their children to demonstrate respect by greeting first to the point of prostrating may meet some resistance (which is understandable). However, children in this context can understand their CaLD parents' viewpoints regarding the expectations and the 'rules' they try to model in the family. It can be challenging, but finding and sustaining the right balance is essential. There may be exceptions, but these situations constitute growing sources of tension in CaLD and multicultural families.

Aside from cultural norms and conflicting expectations, work-family balance is another aspect to explore for wisdom and sustainability.

2.2.2 Family and work

Family and work are fundamental aspects of our well-being as humans. In fact, to most people, they are sides of the same coin. They connect very closely. Most times, they influence each other. But what is the right balance?

When it comes to family, what will you prioritize—work or family? Would a rich family time and, hopefully, strong family connection result in better and sustainable employment? Would more work, higher income, and a better lifestyle result in a more stable family? Some immigrants have been judged as having misplaced priorities when they are perceived to be working long hours at the expense of family time. On the other hand, others have been labelled lazy when they forgo much work (income and lifestyle) because they want to spend more time with the family. So, how can one strike a balance between these inseparable duos?

Parents of CaLD backgrounds are pressured to get out there and work hard to settle the family financially, especially during the early days post-relocation. The typical migrant parent would work longer hours and endure sleepless nights. Soon, they realized so much was happening at the home front without their knowledge or contributions. This chronic disconnection has created family gaps requiring much more effort to bridge down the track. The situation is not made easier by the 'competition' in some CaLD communities. One may be asked: "what have you achieved compared to your contemporaries driving luxurious cars, living in houses, and their children are attending elite schools? Now imagine how this situation is more unsettling when such questions come from your family members, overtly or covertly.

The issue may be further compounded when extended family members back in the home country cast financial burdens on the new immigrant by raising needs that require urgent interventions. They generate and send the fund. Thankfully, foreign currencies often convert to a relatively large sum of money when delivered in less developed countries. But is it ever enough?

Thus, migrant parents caught in such a web would be looking for opportunities to work multiple jobs. They would invest their hearts and energies into tedious work schedules to achieve the level of wealth that would enable them to meet those expectations highlighted in the earlier sections. But at what cost to wellness and family?

CaLD communities are now dealing with some of the longer-term consequences. There are accounts where such *hard-working* migrant parents have reached the other side of their 'achievements,' but only to realise they are alone. They have lost connection with their families. There are even worse cases, with no family left.

It's no secret that some jobs compete significantly with family time. In such a context, children often become teenagers and adults with a disconnect between them and working parents, probably because the latter was not there when they needed them most. This situation is a growing trend amongst CaLD families. Again, this is not hastily apportioning blames. Instead, it is flagging barriers to achieving family sustainability in the context of immigration.

The other aspect of work-related challenges involves difficulties securing employments that match the valued skills and work experiences of CaLD people. Research and statistics have shown that the skills and education of immigrants are often not well valued and utilized. Bankwest Curtin Economic Centre highlighted this reality in their report *Finding A Place To Call Home*.[18] See Figure 2.6 for some highlights.

Figure 2.6: Some Statistics highlighting the
Gaps between Employment Aspirations and Reality

Only 60% of migrants from a non English-speaking background are working in well-matched jobs. Potentially, this represents a substantial opportunity cost to the economy from under-utilised skills.	Migrants born outside the main English-speaking countries are more likely to feel their skills are under-utilised compared to migrants from English-speaking countries and native-born workers.	Achieving a perfect match between the educational qualifications of migrants from non English-speaking backgrounds and the jobs they hold could deliver an extra $6 billion to the economy per year.

This situation has caused many skilled and educated immigrants to embark on unplanned and mostly undesired changes in their career paths. For example, it is not uncommon to encounter a taxi driver with a Ph.D. degree. There are other cases where highly qualified engineers become aged-care workers, cleaners, etc.

---

[18] Bankwest Curtin Economic Centre, Finding A Place To Call Home. Focus on the States Series, Nov 2019 Pp 38-49

The author always qualifies this illustration: firstly, not all skilled immigrants experience the pains of protracted job search. Secondly, Australian-born people with similar qualifications and work experiences also do these jobs. Finally, some of them might have chosen the option for various reasons.

In any case, there is dignity in working and earning an income to care for oneself, family, and other dependants. These workers deserve respect for the courage to embark on such significant lifestyle changes and keep showing up at unplanned and undesired roles and workplaces.

However, the concern is that a critical mass of skilled immigrants is being 'conditioned' to take such 'survival' jobs. They seem to have little or no choice despite their qualifications and desire to work with their full potentials. More specifically, and in the context of this book: what are the implications for families? Would the impact of unmet esteem and self-actualisation needs just dissipate over time? Are the losses possibly being suppressed or repressed with consequences, known or unknown? These questions can trigger further reflections to enable those coming behind to set the right expectations and strategies and those already in the system to make necessary adjustments, all for sustainability in the family unit.

To the migrant parent, you can be more intentional in maintaining a vital connection with family despite work stress or disappointment in the new country. Also, parents need to keep their listening ears open to pick up signals of concerns that affect children and spouses. The family can commit to the priority of family time regardless of the work-life balance challenges they may experience along the way. Remember, one can lose and regain money, but buying back family time has proven more difficult. It's wise to invest in the latter.

2.2.3 Changing dynamics of the family unit

Most migrants desired some status, career, and lifestyle change when relocating, but which of them prepared for the unavoidable change in family dynamics? Are there challenges and pressures on the family unit because of immigration and relocation? Of course!

Not all issues facing CaLD families can be linked to the impact of relocation. However, research, observations, and lived experience have indicated that many people of CaLD backgrounds find it difficult to keep up with the enormity, the divergence, and the pace of change. This lack of preparedness for change is particularly applicable to those from ethnic backgrounds of very traditional family structures. That is all they have always known until relocating to the West.

This book section does not necessarily pronounce judgment, including labelling right or wrong changes. Instead, it highlights the challenges associated with confronting the differences and the actual or potential impacts on the family. While some may have adapted very well, others are not as agile with consequences that often manifest in tension and home challenges. The resulting disruptions in relationships affect families at all levels – husbands and wives, parents and children, siblings, grandparents, etc.

Let's consider this scenario in Australia. The relevant Courts granted forty-nine thousand divorce certificates in 2018 (see Figure 2.7). With 25,000 cases, both parties were born in Australia and 24,000 had at least one of them being a migrant i.e., they were born overseas. Note the decrease in divorce rate amongst people born in Australia between 2017 and 2018. It continues the upward trend for those with one parent born overseas. The explanation for the complete cause of this difference is beyond the scope of this book. The author is not arguing that immigration causes divorce. However, this trend is worth noting (and possibly, tracking) for ongoing efforts to understand causes and effects and possible correlations to relevant immigration profiles.

Figure 2.7: A Snapshot of Trends with Immigration
and Divorces in Australia (2009 - 2018)

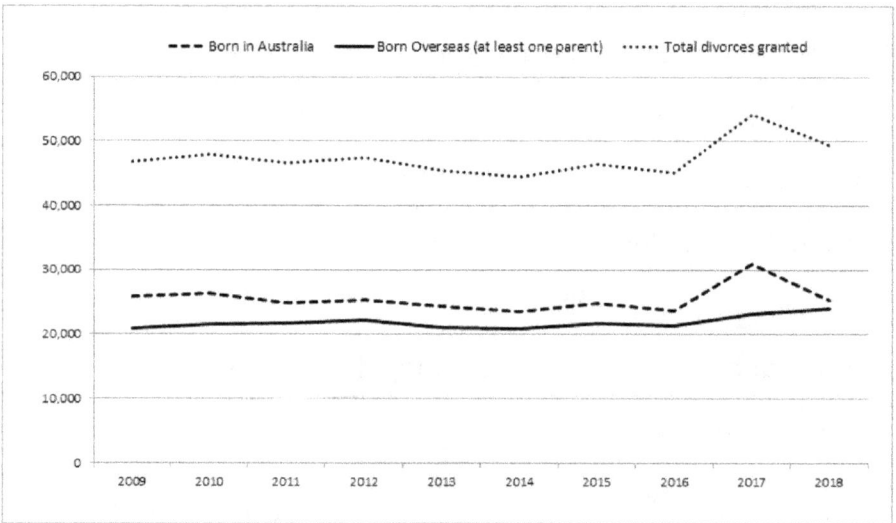

Note: this snapshot is based on the following:
a. **People granted divorce in Australia during the 2009 – 2018 (10 years) period.**[19]
b. **Top 10 countries of birth for overseas-born as of 30 June 2020.**

---

[19] ABS 3310.0 - Marriages and Divorces, Australia, 2018 (Released 27/11/2019 www.abs.gov.au).

Just to re-emphasise, highlighting these statistics are not meant to judge anyone that's separated or divorced. After all, there are situations where it becomes the only safe option. Beyond the numbers and associated analysis, divorce is not an easy terrain. There are deep pains and losses associated with relationship breakdowns. It becomes even more complicated when children are involved. The ripple effects and intergenerational impacts deserve another book. Indeed, such breakdowns would cause trauma of some sort and could significantly impact the mental health of members of the separating family.

The primary concern here is to draw the attention of migrant communities and relevant stakeholders to data that may raise questions about the urgency for the sustainability of the family unit. It should also motivate a revisit of the effectiveness of the coping strategies for the inevitable stress that comes with some aspects of immigration and its impact on families.

2.2.4 Multicultural Families and Mental Health

Our mental health is highly significant; it is as important as our physical health. Unfortunately, the matter has not received the deserved collective and satisfactory focus within migrant, CaLD, and multicultural families and communities. People tend to focus (and mostly, wrongly) on only one aspect of mental health – the illness. But it's more than that. We should not make it all about mental illnesses.

What is mental health? As commonly described by experts (in simple terms): when people are equipped with the required resources and can cope with life stresses, they are mentally healthy. However, not everyone will be able to manage throughout their lives. Thus, some people's mental health starts to deteriorate at some point. It often begins as stress and could continue to mental illness if the issues (stressors) are not addressed on time. There are also findings that some mental health conditions are hereditary and only require life or environmental triggers to bring them to the surface.

Why is this topic crucial in the context of this book? Firstly, the trend of mental illness should trigger a collaborative effort by stakeholders in fostering sustainable solutions, particularly in the family context. Research has indicated that almost half of all Australians will experience mental illness in their lifetime.[20] Half! Secondly, and more disturbingly, many deaths by suicide are attributable to mental illnesses. One can only imagine the trauma associated with suicide deaths in families. Thirdly, and more aligned with the critical message, these statistics are not peculiar to Australian-born residents; they include CaLD and multicultural people and the younger generation. It is not a myth.

The topic of mental illnesses in families and communities has become increasingly important and urgent. However, it is still a sensitive topic amongst culturally diverse people for various reasons, including lack of awareness, the long-standing stigma associated with the illnesses within these cultures, and other issues like religious beliefs, lack of trust in the system, etc. Thankfully, relevant government agencies and community groups have made noticeable efforts in driving awareness, providing culturally appropriate approaches, etc. These efforts are commendable because every loss due to mental illness is too expensive to overlook.

---

[20] Australian Government Productivity Commission – Inquiry Report June 2020

According to WHO, post-traumatic stress, depression, and mood disorders are the most reported mental health issues among migrants.[21] Caused by diverse economic, social, and psychological stressors, mental illness needs more attention under the lens of migrant families and stakeholders to manage this rising concern better and intentionally.

Medical experts like psychologists, psychiatrists, mental health practitioners, family therapists, counsellors, and other relevant health professionals are trained, licensed, and supervised to help people deal with such issues. Governments in most western countries also fund organisations wholly dedicated to providing specialist and emergency support regarding mental illnesses. These are the popular ones in Australia:

Lifeline (www.lifeline.org.au) is a non-profit organisation that provides free, 24-hour telephone crisis support services in Australia. Volunteer crisis supporters provide suicide prevention services, mental health support, and emotional assistance, not only via telephone but face-to-face and online. Their Tel: 131114.

---

[21] https://www.euro.who.int/en/health-topics/health-determinants/migration-and-health/migration-and-health-in-the-european-region/10-facts-on-refugee-and-migrant-health/mental-health

Beyond Blue (www.beyondblue.org.au) is an Australian mental health and wellbeing support organisation. They provide support programs to address issues related to depression, suicide, anxiety disorders, and other related mental illnesses. Their Tel: 1800 512 348.

Headspace (www.headspace.org.au) provides early intervention mental health services to younger people, 12-25-year-olds. They help young people, and their family and friends access vital support, including delivering services through their centres situated within communities across Australia. They do online and phone counselling services, vocational services, and outreaches in schools. Their national Office Tel: (03) 9027 0100.

Kids Helpline (www.kidshelpline.com.au) is a free Australian telephone and online counselling service for children and youth aged 5 and 25. Their Tel: 1800 55 1800.

Similar Government-funded and charitable organisations would be in most western countries as readers may want to explore this subject matter a bit more, within their own contexts. Indeed, this book has explored some areas of life that may trigger readers' emotional and mental aspects. Please contact any of these organisations within your respective countries for immediate and reliable help.

However, members of CaLD communities are often reluctant to access these available services for reasons explained in an earlier section. Unfortunately, research has not shown significant change in behaviours and positive actions towards a better uptake of consultations and treatment. Nevertheless, stakeholders can increasingly destigmatise the subject by safely engaging in everyday, intentional, and consistent conversations and actions for enhancing and sustaining the mental health and well-being of CaLD families and communities.

Yet again, this is not to judge anyone; mental illnesses are complex. However, we cannot keep burying our heads in the sand and denying the reality amongst CaLD families and communities. All stakeholders can do more to reduce the occurrence of suicide and other outcomes of mental illnesses in our communities, across all age groups, and in every way possible. Getting this right is critical for sustainability in families, including those of CaLD backgrounds.

2.3 Key Lessons and Considerations for Sustainability

The benefits and challenges presented in the earlier sections of this book set the platform for some thoughts on key lessons that can sustain culturally diverse families in the context of immigration. These lessons are based on the author's lived experiences, research, and significant work with diverse communities. While they are presented in the context of immigrant, CaLD, and multicultural families, some of the principles apply to any family unit.

2.3.1 There Are Many Sides to a Coin

What comes to mind when you think about the 'sides' of a coin? Two sides - back and front? Could there be more than two, with a closer look? What about the edges that go round the coin? Have you thought about it as a third side? Consider the argument that a 20 Australian cents coin has as many as 14 sides (see Figure 2.8 for a snapshot).

Figure 2.8: The many sides of a coin

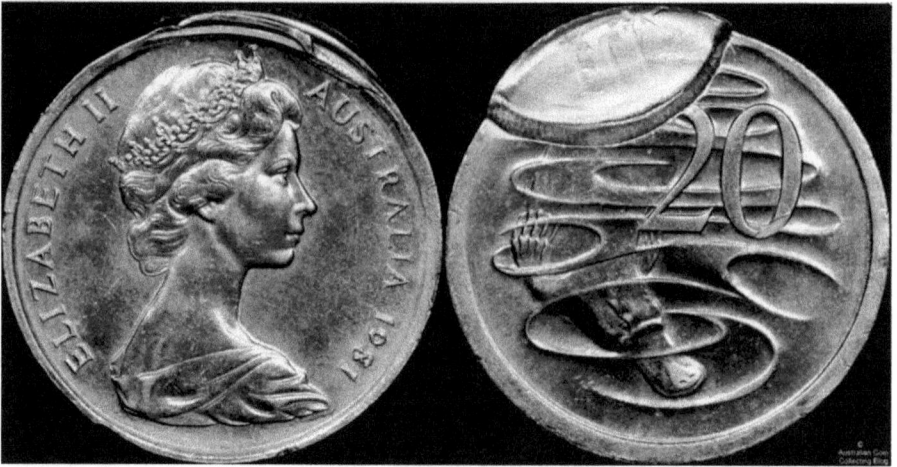

You would ask: how can there be 14 sides? This argument is almost unimaginable indeed. But consider the front, the back, and the multiple edges that run around it continuously. Have you also considered the layered sides inside the coin?

This illustration aims not to teach mathematics, psychology, or philosophy. Moreover, none of these constitute part of the author's areas of strength, anyway. Instead, the critical point is to trigger a reflective exercise in exploring the reality of many sides to a story, an experience, a person, or life in general. This could make room for more patience, empathy, and inclusiveness in families, communities, and other stakeholders when dealing with culturally diverse families.

Back to the Australian 20 cents coin: the metallic object results from a series of complex processes. Iron ore is mined in its raw state from the ground. The 'ugly' ore is put through several refinery methods, including the use of mechanical and chemical reagents and high temperatures and pressures. The final product is the beautifully designed and crafted coin that we see and use. Often, they have images of famous people, landmarks, or other such significant emblems. The head of Queen Elizabeth is on this 20 cents coin. Can you imagine the process it takes to produce the coin? There is more indeed to the story of a coin. How about people and families if there could be such complex and multifaceted steps to produce a coin? How about culturally diverse families. How many sides could there be?

There are many sides to people. How incomplete to judge culturally diverse only by their looks or what the media says! People come in different colours, shapes, smells, etc. What could we be missing or misjudging if we don't take the time and effort to consider the many sides? Their personalities, preferences, skills, etc. There are also many sides to their upbringing and life experiences and the not-so-easy-to-talk-about aspects. 'One size does not fit all' for culturally diverse families!

Yes, migrant people and families are driven to embark on the significant move of relocating to the West for economic prosperity, a better life for family, a higher standard of living conditions, etc. They are also endowed with remarkable talents, skills, and entrepreneurship that can enhance productivity for companies and economic development for nations. They bring very rich cultures that can add value to existing communities. They may struggle to fit in initially, but their resilience will help them to adjust and succeed, maybe with a bit of support in some instances.

Like their fellow humans, members of culturally diverse communities experience physical and mental illnesses at various degrees during their lifetimes. They may not see it as others do. Still, they are open to learning, adjusting, and enjoying a high life expectancy as much as reasonably practicable. There are many sides to our stories. CaLD people themselves should treasure their diversity. Other stakeholders (policymakers, support workers, employers, colleagues, neighbours, etc.) can also appreciate and celebrate this value. We often get maximum benefits when we anticipate and engage the fuller side of people.

2.3.2 The Multiculturality Factor

People of diverse cultural backgrounds differ based on their genes, environments, upbringing, etc. Usually, people do not change every way and react to everything the same way. Therefore, while there is a need for some changes, society should not put them under undue pressure to change who they are just to fit in.

Rather than buying into the negative narratives associated with immigration and cultural diversity, stakeholders can rethink multiculturality in people, families, and communities and the value it brings to all. This value can be acknowledged and harnessed for the greater good of the wider community and professional sectors.

Multicultural teams are increasingly the norms for businesses and projects in most regions of the world. Few commonly reported challenges associated with culturally diverse teams include mistrust, miscommunication, tension, decreased team cohesion, and unproductive time and efforts in dealing with differences. However, researchers and practitioners have primarily agreed that the benefits outweigh such downsides. Multiculturality enhances creativity and competitiveness, solves demand issues for labour, and facilitates new beneficial ways of responding to changing market conditions. It also helps organisations be ready for the future of work that is anticipated to be increasingly diverse and global.[22]

Multiculturality is also significant at the community level, especially in a multicultural society like Australia, which comprises diverse families from different countries, cultures, ethnicities, upbringing, generations, etc. The diversity of colour, fashion, food, and way of thinking and doing things can only be more beneficial than challenging. While it is necessary to maintain commonality in law, human rights, equal opportunities, etc., the value in diversity can also be harnessed for the good of all rather than being relegated or avoided, possibly because of lack of vision and courage for balance. Communities that

---

[22] Osaghae & Olatunji (2021): Dynamic Capabilities in Multicultural Project Teams: Conceptual Review, Framework Analysis and Practical Implications. Proceedings of the Construction Business and Project Management Conference; June 24–25; Cape Town. South Africa

embrace cultural differences will be better positioned to obtain the value of having such diversity.

Australia boasts of a relatively peaceful and viable cultural diversity, almost an international template for others to follow. It is undeniable that relevant governmental bodies, policymakers, businesses, and community organisations will need to support diverse families in the context of immigration. However, the most critical drivers for promoting and harnessing the maximum value from multiculturality start with culturally diverse families. They must own the responsibility for their sustainability. Those with big hearts for big-picture thinking are likely to do well in fostering the long-term viability in the context of immigration and resettlement. They will always consider their next generations.

2.3.3 Generational impacts

The points presented in the preceding sections of this book have indicated the reality of culturally diverse youth and children as key stakeholders in the sustainability of families in the context of immigration. Relevant governmental and non-governmental agencies should take intentional and proactive actions to ensure that culturally diverse families are heard and validated.

The issue of an identity crisis amongst culturally diverse children and youth can no longer be *swept under the carpet* or parked aside, hoping that it would sort out itself. This situation could be one of the most urgent things to address to ensure sustainability. How can parents wisely engage with their CaLD children to help them become more grounded in their identities very early in their young lives? On one side, these children and youth are being regularly reassured of their western identity (e.g., as Australians), and rightly so. They are Australian citizens. They go to Australian schools, with Australian friends. Moreover, they often have an Australian accent, etc. But that's just part of their story.

They also have CaLD ethnicity. They have the CaLD gene. They look CaLD, and often, they still have CaLD accents, however reduced. Rather than such priced diversity to be sold to them as a *curse*, CaLD parents and relevant stakeholders can help them to appreciate and actualise the benefits.

How can all stakeholders work together to help these young folks value their diversity rather than deny it? Unfortunately, to their 'hurt.' Identity is a crucial stabilisation factor for anyone! While CaLD parents may not have this challenge (they often know who they are despite holding multiple passports), their children may struggle. One cannot enforce identity. The difference between the upbringing and experiences of parents compared to children, cannot (and shouldn't) be denied or overlooked. It is real! It's a critical factor for sustainability.

Part of the efforts to bridge this generational gap would include closing relevant cultural gaps and values within the family. For example, a few ethnic community organizations teach their children to value and understand the languages and cultures associated with those ethnicities. It is also vital to acknowledge governments' efforts at all levels in promoting and supporting these initiatives, including financial and in-kind funding. CaLD parents can further complement these efforts by creating forums to discuss the intergenerational challenges and support the younger generation. The agenda is not to drive full preference for the ethnic culture over the culture of their western country of birth. Instead, it is promoting their vantage position of being culturally diverse. The young folks may not hear that much from anywhere else but their own families.

CaLD parents must lead the efforts at continuously exploring and implementing actions for supporting the younger folks as early as possible. Once the prevailing culture and norms are set in their subconscious, it is much more difficult to influence them to adopt their diversity at that stage. They can be educated much earlier about the values of their cultural backgrounds, the reason for it, and how it has evolved over the years. An old African proverb states: 'it takes a village to raise a child.' All stakeholders can facilitate the enabling environment and system for younger culturally diverse generations to achieve their highest aspirations.

2.3.4 Immigration Policies: Solution, Barrier, or Neutral?

Before exploring some thoughts about this vital topic, it is necessary to provide a disclaimer due to the nature of immigration. Any information presented in this section is general. It is mainly taken from the Australian Department of Home Affairs website and shouldn't be considered immigration advice. This governmental department administers the Immigration and Citizenship Program. They are also responsible for the migration program planning levels.

There will be equivalent immigration and citizenship departments in most countries. Again, the Australian context serves as our case study.

The size and composition of the migration policies and programs are set, implemented, and managed for pre-determined purposes. For example, Australian immigration is designed to achieve a range of economic and social outcomes, including building the economy, supporting labour market, reuniting families, and shaping society. The Australian Government sets the levels as part of the annual Budget process. It is reported that the Department of Home Affairs consults with State and Territory governments, academia, industry, and community organisations to arrive at these numbers, etc.[23]

The department claims that they consider public submissions, economic and labour forecasts, international research, and net overseas migration as part of the planning process. The website also states (Dec 2021) that the Migration

---

[23] https://immi.homeaffairs.gov.au/what-we-do/migration-program-planning-levels

Program will have an overall planning level of 160,000 places for 2021-22. See Table 2.2 for the breakdown.

Table 2.2: 2021-22 Migration Program planning levels

2021-22 Migration Program planning levels	
Stream and Category	**Places in 2021-22**
Skill stream	
Employer Sponsored	22,000
Skilled Independent	6,500
Regional	11,200
State/Territory Nominated	11,200
Business Innovation & Investment Program	13,500
Global Talent	15,000
Distinguished Talent	200
Skill Total	**79,600**
Family Stream	
Partner	72,300
Parent	4,500
Child (estimate; not subject to a ceiling)	3,000
Other Family	500
Family Total	**80,300**
Special Eligibility	100
Total	**160,000**

Skill stream is designed to support Australia's economy, including filling skill shortages in the labour market. Sponsorship by employers is given more weight amongst the options for skilled migration. The Department has also ramped up its efforts to attract the "brightest and best global talent" to work and live permanently in Australia. This strategy supports the economy by introducing innovative skills to high-priority industries. The overall trend in the skilled stream has remained consistent in the past few years.

The Family stream is our focus for this section and the overall message of this book. Australia's visa program allows Australian citizens and permanent residents to sponsor some partners and family members for temporary or permanent visas. The distribution (Table 2.2) would likely trigger some reflective questions. Why is the program predominantly made up of Partner visas (90%)? Of course, the Australian government reserves the right to channel immigration policies towards the best interest of Australia and Australians as a whole. It shouldn't necessarily be biased towards any group, including CaLD members of the community. Indeed, the family story in the migration program, as depicted in Table 2.2, portrays the position that family reunions will mainly support skilled migration, which ultimately helps build the economy. But sustainability of families, mainly migrant and multicultural families, goes beyond supporting the economy though the latter is also important.

How have such immigration policies contributed to family dynamics, especially when one considers the factors discussed in previous sections of this book? However, it is acknowledged that immigration dynamics are just as complex as managing family dynamics. Imagine dealing with issues that connect the two in some shape and depth; the complexity is further amplified. How about the integration of a third dimension - cultural diversity? These are not easy terrains to navigate, singly or in combination. See Figure 2.9 for the pictorial depiction of the interplay. This chart provides the basis for further illustration.

Figure 2.9: A Depiction of the Vital Interplay between Immigration, Cultural Diversity, and Family

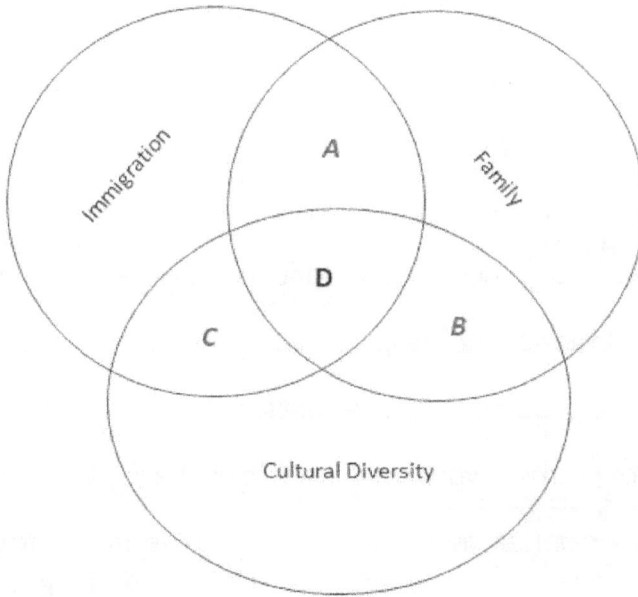

So far in this book, we have dwelt much more in the 'A' and 'B' interfaces related to families. The considerations included exploring some of the beneficial drivers for the big move associated with immigration and some associated challenges whether appreciated during the time of decision or not. We have also considered some aspects of dealing with cultural shocks and conflicts in-house and out there in the community.

Let's consider a few points with the 'A' intersection from an immigration viewpoint. No immigration advice is being offered here. There are specialist immigration lawyers and agents trained and registered for that purpose. However, we can make some points in alignment with the critical message. About 37 types of visas might be suitable for people wanting to join families in Australia.[24] Of course, there are legal validity requirements, eligibility criteria, and conditions associated with the visas. Indeed, no responsible government will leave its borders unprotected or free-for-all. Thus, there is a limited number of family visas granted per year. And they are significantly partner visas. For example, nine in ten family visas planned to be granted during 2021-22 are partner visas. There is considerably less hope for other family reunions, i.e., parents, children, brothers, sisters, or other eligible relatives. Is this going to help with the sustainability of CaLD, multicultural and migrant families? Is there room for governments and policymakers to do more?

The challenges associated with the 'B' intersection typically become more apparent once immigrant families have relocated to the West. There is little any government can do to help resolve this for any family. Integrating into a

---

[24] https://immi.homeaffairs.gov.au/visas/getting-a-visa/visa-finder/join-family

new society with its existing cultural diversity would put more responsibility on the new family to adjust accordingly. It could even be more challenging to deal with the cultural shocks inside family units than outside, as seen in the previous sections of this book. Shifting beliefs and values within the family can be challenging to manage. Adjustments are inevitable for achieving sustainability in migrant and multicultural families.

Arguably, immigration policies can also influence the cultural diversity of a country (intersection 'C'). Could Australian Department of Home Affairs refer to the same concept *shaping society*? Let's briefly take our attention back to an earlier section of this book, *Table 1.1 Australia's population by top 10 countries of birth*. Why are the top 10 countries in the top 10? How would that diversity be shaped going forward? Or rather, would it be maintained as it is into the foreseeable future? Who and what determines this distribution or diversity? How is it determined? The reader would have already figured out that the author does not answer these questions. However, it is a question that may also be close to the hearts of other members of our diverse Australian community. The same considerations would apply in other countries, with immigration an essential aspect of economic and population policies. One thing is sure, though: immigration has a lot to play in shaping society indeed.

What about the convergence of 'D'? One would need more than a book to fully unpack the dynamics of what happens with the interplay between immigration, family, and cultural diversity. Whether immigration policies can be part of the solution or the problem regarding the sustainability of migrant families can be presented as triggers for reflection for stakeholders, including the relevant governmental departments, policymakers, migration lawyers and agents, and the families themselves.

Policymakers can do more in considering the implications in the short, medium, and long terms. For example, why should eligible citizens of a country have to wait for as much as 30 years for outcomes of their applications to sponsor family members to join them? Could there be more that governments and immigration departments can do to lessen the wait time and financial burden of family visa applications? Have we considered the argument that the benefits of such family reunions from timely and affordable visa grants are not just for the sponsors? Their children and following generations are often the key drivers behind such visa applications.

The benefits for children in multicultural and migrant families to experience their root cultures via reunion with other family members in the family tree are arguably incalculable. It would potentially help be grounded in their ethnicity and identity, enhancing their overall stability. Imagine situations where children of CaLD backgrounds can spend quality time with their grandparents or other eligible relatives with the capacity to provide them with relevant cultural grounding.

The urgency for sustainability in multicultural and migrant families deserves actions that may not necessarily wait for immigration and policymakers. Families can take the initiative and take more decisive steps.

2.3.5 Big Picture Thinking and Actions: The Key to Sustainability

Immigrant and multicultural people and families often confront the challenges of culture shocks and conflicts, work-family balance, changing dynamics in the family unit differently. More importantly, how families deal with the situations will determine the length and depth of impact.

Therefore, big picture thinking or doing will be helpful. It pays to start with your *why* again, i.e., your purpose for relocation.

There are significant benefits in articulating and keeping in focus the reason/s for embarking on the substantial change of immigration and permanent relocation to a new country, new culture, new weather, new systems, with no guaranty for success, etc. It is often about a better standard of living for self and family. It could also constitute safety (running from actual or potential harm to self or family), further studies, economic prospects (via work or business), or joining family members. Keeping your *why* freshly in mind will provide extra support for overcoming the challenges discussed in the previous sections. It gives the hinges for digging deep and enjoying stability while facing challenges.

It is also essential to do the big picture thinking and positioning, not just one-off, but on an ongoing, sustainable basis. For example, how would immigrant families survive even for a season when confronted with the challenges of culture shocks and conflicts, work-family balance, and changing family dynamics? How would they maintain balance, including choosing the battles to fight, letting others go by, and keeping hope alive? On-going refocusing and readjusting expectations would be required for survival and sustainability.

CaLD families can strive to stay and grow together and build trust in one another as early as possible. The chance of attaining the latter can be enhanced if all family unit members are aligned with the whys in the first instance. They must keep working together as a team to achieve these shared goals. People hardly fight for what they don't own. Proactive and selfless leadership would help ensure shared ownership of the purpose for relocation, as much as reasonably practicable.

It is vital to proactively recognise and work hard to avoid blind spots that can cause disharmony in the family, including the challenges presented in the earlier sections of this book. Look out for one another and yourself as an individual (self-care). Surround yourself with a caring community rather than trying to do life alone. Also, seek help from professionals where necessary. They have the training and supervision to help families, especially during those trying periods in life's journey. Your family is worth the fight!

The author presents some points targeted at the men in families in the next chapter. This action is not placing more importance on men, but, firstly, because the author is a man (he can relate). Secondly, helping one family member ultimately helps sustain the entire unit. Finally, the statistics about men's wellbeing trigger urgent attention and care by all stakeholders.

Chapter 3

Multicultural Men: Adopt, Adapt, Or Abandon!

There is a sense of urgency and attention for migrant and multicultural men. There are increasing reports and statistics of traumatic events and experiences often related to immigration and family life in the West. A few of the stories, including leading and lagging causes, have been highlighted in earlier sections of this book.

Considering the significant benefits already described, it doesn't make much sense to make a case for abandoning the immigration project altogether. However, the option presents a potential for reducing the impact in scenarios where relocating, settling, or residing in the West do not go well.

The entire family unit feels the impacts of challenges in family life. However, men, fathers, husbands, and male partners deserve a unique focus. Reports and statistics have shown that men are at the core of the causes and effects of many of the challenges in culturally diverse families, rightly or wrongly. As the other family members adjust quickly, the men persist for various reasons. Here are some insights based on observations, research, and lived experiences.

Dealing with work-related stress

Let's consider the impact of employment. CaLD men would typically be out in the market, hunting jobs, especially in the early days of settling into the new country. That comes with varying degrees of impact depending on individual family context. Research and experience show that they are often unsuccessful in securing their desired employment.

Wang and Jing (2018) conducted one such research. Their study examined the level of job satisfaction among immigrant workers and found out that, for the most part, the majority are not satisfied with the work they do. Many immigrant men work as a means of survival, not as a desired career or life goal.[25] This point is not to discourage anyone but to highlight reality while encouraging more preparations for the challenges ahead.

Now imagine how this work/career scenario chisels off a man's psyche, ego, and sense of self? Consider the uncertainties with income, loss of professional esteem, and all

---

[25] Job Satisfaction Among Immigrant Workers: A Review of Determinants. Jhongmin Wang and Xinlin Jing (2018)

the associated traumas. If not well controlled, this situation, transfers to loss of respect at home, tension of various ramifications, and other impacts.

Change in Family Dynamics

There are significant changes in family dynamics for CaLD people when they move from their traditional cultural backgrounds to the western world. The effect is not currently appreciated as it should. The traditional role of men as breadwinners is changing. It is now a shared responsibility regarding decision-making, financial management, housework, childcaring, etc. The functions are even reversed in some cases.

Respect has taken on a new meaning. Children may no longer greet parents first, contrary to the norm in the upbringing of many CaLD men. Moreover, children may not necessarily depend on parents financially as they may have options, where necessary. CaLD men do not particularly cope so well losing the positioning where other family members are dependent on them. They have often grown up in traditional settings where such dependency is valued as an indication of their "'manhood' and correlates to their social status in the family and society.

We saw the alarming divorce rate, including marriages involving CaLD people in Australia (see Figure 2.7 in an earlier section). Of course, divorce affects everyone in the family, including the separating couples themselves, children, friends, extended family, and generations ahead. Again, research has shown that men do not particularly do well in failed marriages and broken relationships in the family. Let's use some statistics in Australia about mental health, suicide, and family relationships (see Figure 3.1) to illustrate this point further. Three thousand deaths were due to suicide in 2018; an average of 8+ deaths per day (mostly men); *81% of this mortality is attributed to relationship breakdown.*

Figure 3.1: A snapshot of key statistics relating to men and the impact of mental illness

- 3000+ deaths due to suicide in 2018 (3,046)
- 8+ deaths each day by suicide in Australia on average (8.4)
- 6.4 males per day, 2 females per day
- 75% of suicide deaths were men in Australia (2,320)
- 81.0% of suicides due to relationship breakdown are men
- Each year, around 100,000 Australians attempt suicide
- It is estimated that more than 500,000 Australians have attempted suicide at some time in their life.

posted by pbb on September 10, 2020

Does seeing these stats do something to you? Does it make you pause for a while to reflect? Even if you are not a man, you have a man in your life, presumably a father, brother, uncle, boyfriend, husband, partner, colleague, etc. It is not just about men; everyone should be concerned. 'We're in it together.

It's not just about men; who wins?

Who wins with all these challenging situations and alarming statistics? This situation should drive big-picture thinking that's necessary for sustainability. There is an urgent need for change which CaLD men can lead. After all, they have a lot at stake. They are likely to be significantly impacted by a breakdown in family relationships. See Figure 3.1 again for the numbers!

Indeed, this section does not promote men as more important, or support destructive behaviours like domestic violence, etc. It's aimed at helping to position CaLD men as an agency for change and sustainability in the family. There are no true winners when families are dysfunctional, and the situation takes significant physical and mental health toll on all parties involved, including men.

Unfortunately, some CaLD men have attempted to take matters into their hands in the wrong way. The need to obey the law is not debatable in keeping the balance. Some men who thought beating up partners, wives, or kids was okay have been prosecuted in the past. It is not okay! It is called family and domestic violence in Western Australia, for example. Committing such an offence is punishable under the law, and offenders may end up in jail with criminal records that are almost impossible to delete.

Who wins if one of the members of the family goes to jail? Even if no one ends up in jail, what about the psychological injury of domestic violence? Consider another potential result of such situations at home, i.e., the child is taken away from the parents and placed in a foster home. Who wins? The statistics of the life outcomes of children that grow up without a father in their lives are all over the public domain. Who wins? Even if you are granted a divorce in court, you win custody of children, or you win a court ruling on most or all assets, is that real victory? Sustainability makes it possible for all parties to win together.

We have this remarkable quote in a bestselling book titled *Things Fall Apart* by Chinua Achebe: "things fall apart the centre cannot hold."[26] Balance is typically achieved when the foundation is right. Getting the foundation right is not what any governmental agency, community groups, lawyers, mediators, etc., can do for a family. Instead, family members themselves would have to do this themselves. The earlier this is done, the better it is for the whole family unit. Families give themselves the best chance for balance when they stay committed to these foundational aspects of the unit. The incentives are there for men to lead this commitment.

Marriage takes two to tango. Two with shared core beliefs, shared values, and shared commitments. This deep alignment provides a high chance of success that will keep the balance despite the growing odds against the family. However, finding that balance takes much more than the foundations. It takes the two to keep working together, even before the children come and go, along the journey. It is about sustainability. Again, men can lead. But it takes two to maintain. It becomes tricky when things no longer hold together despite efforts from one or both parties. Unpacking the complexities and intricacies in

---

[26] Achebe C. (1994): Things Fall Apart. Doubleday, New York

marriage separation and divorce is beyond the scope of this book despite its relevance to the critical message. However, the stats did show that men do not do so well with the fall-out. The need for self-care, including mental health care, has become evident for sustainability in the CaLD families.

Meanwhile, it seems like CaLD men have taken an oath of silence about mental health issues. There appears to be a prevalent pretence that it is not an issue if it's not close to one's corridors or right in one's family. But numbers don't lie (see Figure 3.1 again). Thankfully, there's been a bit of shift in momentum as some key stakeholders, community groups, and services providers are pushing for more open conversations about it, positively and ethically. Many research programs, educational activities, and community initiatives are being implemented to help men talk more about mental health issues. Such proactive interventions can stop endangering situations from leading to significant damages like suicide.

The author feels a sense of urgency towards the need for CaLD men to adopt and adapt to enhance their wellbeing in settling and living in the West, including the context of family life. He also argues for the option to abandon the project of immigration if they are not ready for change.

3.1 Adopt

CaLD families now residents in the West must take decisive steps to blend well, both in heart and action, to make things work for them, their families, and their generations to come.

Consider the adoption of a non-biological child into your family and raising the child as your own. Indeed, there were other children in the home before the adoption who you cannot (and should not) deny. Instead, you love all family members. When you come in and settle into a new country in the West, you would (and should), as a necessity, adopt new laws, new cultures, new experiences, etc. Some are excellent and enjoyable, others a bit more challenging.

However, this adoption does not mean that you deny all your upbringing, roots, and identity. Indeed, expect some form of evolution and blending over time. The target is to strike the right balance for you and your family within boundaries like the law, personal capacity, family dynamics, etc.

3.1.1 Culture is dynamic

Did anyone expect that cultures would remain the same over the years? No! They change over time, even in countries where indigenes have managed to preserve their traditional cultures for generations. What were the expectations of CaLD people when they relocated from their countries of upbringing to settle in new countries where culture(s) already existed?

For instance, when a family in the neighbourhood invites you for dinner in Australia, you are generally expected to "bring a plate" along. That means you would bring some type of food to share with your host as well. The other typical example entails expecting you to pay for your meal or drinks when work colleagues invite you for lunch. Thus, what do you do as a new immigrant who has grown up in a different culture (i.e., one that practices that you should make adequate provision for all)?

Would you expect your culture to be dominant when you relocate and reside in a new country? What about the cultures already existing in the place? Is it not better to hope that they would make room for your own culture, at best?

What if you (and others practicing the same culture as yours) are in the minority? Is this not a valid case for adopting new cultures while continuing to cherish and practice yours as much as reasonably practicable?

Members of CaLD communities are increasingly realising that things are no longer the way they left them back in their places of upbringing. Everyday living has changed drastically over time. Even the most traditional cultures are changing. Moreover, how can cultures remain relevant to the younger generations, including those born in the new countries of residence, different from their country of ancestry? Culture, by necessity, must become dynamic to be sustainable. The dynamism would also extend to the people associated with the cultures.

The flipside of the argument is also valid: people should not be pressured to change too quickly. More seriously, they 'shouldn't be pushed to forgo their valued cultural upbringing and identities. The issues of identity crises may become more problematic than those associated with lack of integration if we 'don't strike the right balance. Stakeholders can support CaLD people to continue practicing their cultures while adopting the new cultures, all within the boundaries of humanity and the law.

Many research programs have indeed highlighted the need for some form of acculturation - changes in values and behaviours individuals make to accommodate the culture of in their new settlement. The study in Norway was one of them. [27] The researchers argued that acculturation addresses two underlying dimensions: the degree to which one's heritage culture is maintained and the degree to which one wishes to participate and contact other cultural groups. They concluded that immigrants who adopt the majority culture are likely to be more optimistic about seeking help from public health services than those who do not. These findings could explain why culturally diverse families may not access the available mental health services, which could continue to have significant ramifications.

CaLD men can be part of the solution. They can provide the leadership for handling culture shocks and conflicts so that it gets better for all members of the family unit. Such positive steps may involve making provisions for cultural

---

[27] Markova V. Sandal G. M. and Pallesen S. (2020) Immigration, acculturation, and preferred help-seeking sources for depression: comparison of five ethnic groups)

dynamism as all family members settle into the rhythms of integrating into a new society and experiences. Culture is dynamic.

3.1.2 Shared Rights, Respect, and Responsibilities

Sharing respect, responsibilities, decision-making, and leadership with other members of the family unit is one of the challenging areas for CaLD men. A significant number of these men have made noticeable efforts to shift from the traditional culture of their upbringing. However, they would also need to adopt the prevailing western culture as fast as required to ensure the sustainability of their family.

In some shape and form, the system in the West provides a heightened awareness for children to know their rights concerning anyone, including parents. They know their rights to be respected irrespective of whether the other party may be their senior sibling, uncle, aunt, grandparent, or even a parent. The children know that using a harsh tone when addressing them could be disrespectful. Whether openly done or not, there is also the perception regarding the justification for them to greet you first as a parent.

The other common practice in the West, which has been challenging to adopt, entails situations where children or younger folks call older adults by their first names. This practice is against the traditional norm in most CaLD communities. The expectation is for them to address elderly folks of your parent's age as 'aunty' or 'uncle.' There have been cases where children challenged parents that have attempted to maintain this tradition in the West. They would protest: *"But he's not my uncle"* or something along that line. This same argument applies to situations relating to timing and choice of children's tertiary education, whether they would marry or not, who they could marry, etc. Their rights and respect for their choices are becoming a critical determinant on the way forward with sustainability.

The author will not extensively discuss the issue of physical discipline like smacking or using a stick on a child to *teach them a lesson*. Any CaLD man that still does that, however discrete he may have been, would get into trouble soon. The potential for jail (or at least losing his children to foster care) is almost inevitable. God help you if you leave a mark on the child, however unintentional! CaLD men must find other ways to discipline and achieve the intended results. This aspect of the message in this book is one where there is no debate; stop being physical like smacking, caning, etc.

Could there be an argument that society in the West is 'pushing too much unto the 'plates' of children and younger generations without thinking of the more significant implications? Was the traditional family structure providing a form of safety that no other system can provide? Are children increasingly put in the driving seat for a journey they may not have been well prepared to lead? Are they ready for the responsibilities associated with critical decisions? Some form of balance always provides better stability, primarily when related to such a sensitive and most fragile matter.

The situation is further compounded for CaLD men, who typically will have to deal with the challenges of relocation and lead the family to start life all over, both in parallel. They would also strive to overcome the hurdles along the path of establishing their place in the socio-economic fabric of the new location. Keeping the family together (in harmony) while developing stable roots for generational growth in the new residence is essential for sustainable family experiences. They must be ready to share rights, respect, and responsibilities, particularly to the extent necessary for the sustainability of their families. Unfortunately, these family-related challenges significantly affect CaLD men, including their mental health. If not addressed early and correctly, they also face the risk of more severe outcomes (see Figure 3.1 again). Meanwhile, despite instances of the need in applicable cases, CaLD men have been widely reported as the least likely to seek help to preserve their mental health or deal with mental illness.

3.1.3 Mental health is too human to remain a stigma

It is almost intuitive that some of the challenges facing CaLD men, as presented in this book so far, would likely cause trauma. The need for mental health care is virtually inevitable. It is not uncommon to hear reports of homesick cases, especially for new arrivals. There is also the endemic issue of unemployment and loss of careers due to relocation. The loss of identity or conflicts therein is less discussed, even though it could be as damaging as other traumatic experiences. All forms of separation in the family unit — parent-children, siblings, husband-wife, etc. will typically result in some form of distress, and sometimes, more severe issues.

Just like we proactively and actively care for our physical health (and we should), we ought to do the same for our mental wellbeing. Issues pushed away or 'swept under the carpet' either because of procrastination, shame, or lack of understanding, do not get sorted by themselves. They would resurface later, in some form, and often more traumatic and more widespread. It is usually better to resolve them in the first instance.

However, mental health with association of 'craziness' is still prevalent in some CaLD communities. This type of belief is another indication that people usually do not just change their mindsets that easily. It may take time and even generations to displace, replace, or integrate such views with other proven facts of life. So much stigma is still associated with mental health illnesses, unfortunately. The follow-on effect of that is the unhealthy silence about the matter. Thus, there is a scarcity of data that would have helped to provide information for long-term planning for prevention and recovery measures within culturally diverse communities. The situation is further compounded for CaLD men because the belief that 'men 'don't 'cry' and 'don't show their vulnerability has further constituted significant barriers to seeking timely help where necessary.

Just like it is common knowledge that men typically delay seeking medical help for physical ailments, the situation may be the same for mental health. Thus, issues go undetected for a long time, and it only shows up later as a disaster waiting to happen. Basic knowledge of physics taught us that things kept under pressure over a long time would explode. Men, including CaLD men, must learn to talk — at least to the extent that things do not explode. Indeed, an explosion causes more severe and broader damages with lasting impacts. The family is the last place we want to have such damaging blasts. CaLD men can position themselves better to avoid such situations and ensure sustainable family experiences. Mental health is too human to remain a stigma. Men must lead the change they want to see, not just for themselves only, but for the good of the entire family unit, as much as reasonably possible.

3.2 Adapt

Change often involves adaptation. For the context of this book, this entails making some adjustments that are suitable to the requirements or conditions of residing in a new place with your family and generations ahead. Adaptation is necessary for sustainability. It's often stated that the dinosaur became extinct because they didn't change (or adapt). In contrast, the walking birds adapted by growing wings over time. They learned how to fly and survived being hunted into extinction. The dinosaurs died off despite their size.

The statistics already showed disturbing trends of men dying earlier. Could there be lessons from the story of the dinosaur? Could the women have learned to adapt like the birds and secured the secret to living longer? Again, this is not necessarily promoting gender competition here. Instead, it is challenging for CaLD men to take time to reflect on how much they've adapted since relocation. Immigration is a significant change in life. It deserves an intentional approach regarding settling in and achieving the purpose for the big move.

The point has been made in previous sections of this book: people do not (and shouldn't be pressurised to) change who they are, i.e., their identity. The latter is a major foundational piece of any human, even when their upbringing has involved painful experiences. A foundation provides structure, strength, and stability. Yes, some foundations may need some form of rework, fortification, or even replacement of some parts. However, it is critical to preserve one's foundational identity, including the family unit and its individuals. Thus, adaptation does not necessarily imply changing everything and losing one's identity. Doing the latter could arguably contribute to the cause of identity crisis and the root causes of some issues associated with CaLD families. But the other extreme of sticking to one's old and traditional ways (like the dinosaur) could be as costly. A call for change goes out to all CaLD men, at least for the sake of the sustainability of their families.

Culture is dynamic, and CaLD men must lead their families to adapt and work with the prevailing dynamism. It is laudable for these men to try to preserve relevant cultural practices associated with their upbringing (and that worked well for them). However, they must also be ready to adjust, including letting go of what's not working for their new realities in the new place. With a collectivist background, 'when you invite people over for a meal or drink, you make adequate provision for everyone.' However, when you resettle into an individualist culture (which is the case with most western countries), people expect individuals to bring something to share or some money to contribute to the meal. Some CaLD people may only need to adjust to the extent necessary. Moreover, this may take more time for some than others.

The matter of sharing rights and respect with other members of the family unit is not a matter of debate, nor is it typically open to cultural interpretations or preferences. For example, the physical discipline of a child is based on the mindset "you will spoil a child when you spare the rod." The other example is the belief that "a spouse must always obey irrespective of the husband's actions." Men with such mindsets may end up in jail. Would you rather be the dinosaur that's locked away or, like the bird, adapt and fly above the challenges?

Mental health is too human to remain a stigma. With a forecast that "almost half of all Australians will experience mental illness at some point in their life,"[28] more people are beginning to accept the reality and talk more about their mental health. Thankfully, CaLD men are adapting and talking about this matter though the pace can be better. This shift is particularly significant because they have often come from a cultural background where mental illness is still considered a "curse." People suffering from the disease are ostracised as "mental" or crazy. They are often institutionalised (if their families can afford the exorbitant cost). It is worse for others that are not so lucky or 'privileged," and they are pushed onto the street where, unfortunately, many die from hunger, disease, assault, car accidents, etc. CaLD men living in the West must continue to adapt as necessary. They must embrace and promote mental health awareness and valuable conversations associated with the matter. Increasingly, they must champion actions that will destigmatise the issue.

CaLD men can adapt and thrive like the bird. Is it often easy to change? No. Again, like the bird, one can do it over

---

[28] Australian Government Productivity Commission Inquiry Report June 2020

time, if necessary. Shed some old wings that have become barriers. Preserve some that are helpful. Grow new ones that are required for strength and flight. Then fly well. Adaptation is necessary for sustainability. The alternative is to abandon the project of relocating and settling into life and permanent residence in the West (along with your family). Abandonment may present a better option than ending up like the dinosaur.

3.3 Abandon

In the author's best-selling book,[29] he explored the Triple A guide of Adopt Adapt Achieve with a significant focus on careers for CaLD people and skilled immigrants. He drove his message towards a positive end of achieving one's goals for immigration. The same logic applies to the context of this current book on immigration and family sustainability. You will most likely achieve your family sustainability goals by following the correct integration principles. As presented in earlier sections of this book, the information and guidelines associated with adoption and adaptation will work for you if you apply them properly.

Realistically, not everyone, including CaLD people, would take all these necessary steps for achieving their goals. It may

---

[29] Adopt Adapt Achieve: An Amazing Triple A Guide for Successful Relocation, Change and Integration (amazon.com.au)

be better to abandon the project and explore other alternatives to relocation to the West than facing the prospect of tension, separation in the family, risk of incarceration, potential ill health, and the associated trauma for all family members. Avoidance is better than years of regrets, remedies, and recovery.

However, multicultural men are typically known to be resilient. They would keep hope alive and continue to do all they can to preserve the harmony and sustainability of their families.

Chapter 4

Future Projections

People and families migrate having a future in mind—a lot filled with hopes and aspirations worthy of the effort required to succeed. Of course, many CaLD and multicultural families derive significant benefits from relocating and settling into western societies. However, they also experience challenges along the way.

This section highlights some projected scenarios for the future regarding CaLD families in the context of immigration and resettlement. Some recommendations for sustainability would be offered, as applicable. Figure 4.1 matrix provides some illustration.

Figure 4.1: Future Scenarios and Decision-Implications Matrix

	Stay	Leave
Change	A	B
No Change	C	D

This matrix is based on the principles presented in earlier sections of this book, including the benefits, challenges, and critical lessons of relocation to the West. Users would maximise their understanding if they adequately read and reflected on the previous points. Here is a brief description of the various future scenarios:

Stay:

The CaLD family (one or more members) remains in the new place of residence.

Leave:

The CaLD family leaves and goes back to their country of origin. They abandoned the project of resettling along with the goals that drove the decision to relocate in the first instance.

Change:

The CaLD family (one or more members) adopts and adapts to the extent necessary for sustainability.

No Change:

The CaLD family does not adopt nor adapt, and they do not intend to do so.

To reiterate, the objectives of these projections are not necessarily to judge any of these decisions. Instead, the intention is to highlight critical areas for considerations and potential implications of such choices.

Now, to explain the different quadrants A to D in the matrix:

A. Stay and Change

This quadrant is the ideal status that CaLD families would want to achieve sooner than later. They are staying and reconciling the fact that the new place of residence is now home. Thus, they are making intentional and tangible efforts to adopt and adapt *like the bird*.

Hopefully, all members of the family unit are aligned with this positioning, and they grow and achieve their goals together. They've reached a balanced rhythm in working with the current dynamism of culture - a synchronisation of their ancestral roots, alignment on the prevailing culture of the new place of residence, and their preferences, going forward. They've also struck the right balance for shared rights, respect, and responsibilities. They are most likely to enjoy reasonably good health, including mental wellbeing.

B. Leave and Change

The CaLD family in this position would have implemented the necessary changes as much as they could. However, their experiences so far could have already done the damage. They would still decide to leave and return to their country of origin. Hopefully, the lessons learned would provide some benefits to take with them.

C. Stay and No Change

This is a situation where the family remained in the new residence in the West but did not make any change (and they are not willing to do so). If not checked, members of the family unit will likely continue to be exposed to the risk of cultural conflicts, the tension in the home, separation at all levels, domestic violence, incarceration, and mental illnesses.

Of course, there could be other moderating factors like time, i.e., other external factors may change with time that could force changes in the family. Unfortunately, this leaves the situation to chance, which does not ensure sustainability in the family unit irrespectively of where they reside.

D. Leave and No Change

The CaLD family in this quadrant goes back to their country of origin (singly or some form of combination, together). They also do not make any change while in the new country in the West. They refuse to learn any lesson from the experience.

Thus, as they are not doing well in the new country, they may likely not do well back in their home country because they would have to confront the issues. Some statistics and demographic studies have shown the global generational shifts in culture, demand for shared rights, respect, and responsibilities, for example, are now prevalent in many regions of the world.

It is worth highlighting that the scenarios above may not apply to all members of the family unit, the same way, all the time. Indeed, the laws in western countries can facilitate such individualistic actions. For example, the CaLD father/husband/male partner may be the only one resisting change or deciding to leave. Other members of the unit may choose not to go with him. The reverse is also true but less common.

In such cases, the law would likely protect the rights of the other members of the family unit to choose to stay or leave. Thus, the fruits from the seed of separation may become evident even with family members spreading across geographical regions, often with unresolved and deep-rooted conflicts and brokenness. Unfortunately, these manifestations may proceed into generations ahead. Therefore, big-picture views and actions are necessary when confronting such family-related issues at all levels and phases.

Considerations Beyond the Matrix

There are situations where the scenarios would not be distinctly situated within a quadrant. For example, the family could be in between A and B, i.e., they want to stay and leave at the same time due to the challenges of resettlement and integration into life in the new country. The author referred to this situation as *a tension of the middle* in one of his other books.[30] Most immigrants would have experienced this situation at some time along the pathway of relocating and settling into a new country. People experience the challenges

---

[30] Voices from Home: Wisdom from Our Diasporic Roots (amazon.com.au)

while enjoying the benefits of living in the western world at the same time.

New mothers feel the loss of missing out in culturally appropriate care that is traditionally enjoyed during such a significant part of their lives – giving birth and first few post-natal days. But they are often thankful for the world-class medical care and new parents' benefits received as a resident of rich western countries. The employment situation of new skilled immigrants is another example that demonstrates this tension. While many often suffer the loss of high-flying careers which they left to reside in the West, they also openly appreciate the high standard of living including relative assurance of security and world-class amenities.

This tension creates mixed feelings in enjoying the benefits and facing the challenges at the same time. Which one goes deeper would depend on the individual and personality, their family dynamics, the prevailing circumstances in the West and back in their home country, etc. These factors would also drive the how long they remain in this position and how quickly they decide to *stay* or *go*, as per the Figure 4.1 matrix.

Most CaLD families would likely situate between A and C. When people stay, they often do not entirely change, nor change everything. That is the more realistic situation. While they embrace the need to change (adopt and adapt), first-generation immigrants cannot wholly 'kill' their cultures of upbringing, even if they attempt to do that. They will always bear the influences and marks of their birthplaces and cultural backgrounds. This type of grounding should be encouraged for the benefits of being well-rooted in one's identities and the advantages. Even children of CaLD people still carry the influences one way or the other, though not as deep and extensive as their parents. The key is to strike the right balance to thrive and be sustainable.

Chapter 5

Concluding Remarks

This book has presented the benefits and challenges in the significant experience of immigration in the context of immigrant, multicultural, culturally diverse, and CaLD families. Hopefully, readers are convinced about the considerable progress that relocation to the West brings to families, including economic prosperity, higher standard of living, and real options for the future of all family unit members.

It is also essential to consider the challenges of immigration when planning to relocate, while settling in, and even later, as residents of the new country. Overlooking the facts does not resolve issues. Every family deserves the correct and current information for creating strategies for sustainable progress and the right balance.

Fortunately, several community groups and service providers support new families relocating to the West. This welcomed trend is likely to continue since immigration is still the preferred policy for supporting the labour market and building the economy for most western nations. The efforts would need to be more targeted and result oriented regarding sustainability in families.

A word to Policymakers

Hopefully, this book has provided a balanced perspective deserving of immigration and family sustainability. Policymakers can obtain additional cultural intelligence from this book to develop more sustainable immigration policies relevant to culturally diverse families.

Policymakers and relevant government departments can do more to understand and validate the genuine aspirations of CaLD people and the barriers they face. People are motivated by needs. They would feel more supported when their goals are kept alive and achieved. People relocated via the humanitarian visa pathway does not necessarily mean that they don't have higher-level goals. While continuing to make budgetary allowances and award grants at various levels, governmental efforts can be more tangible, more culturally appropriate, and more sustainable, especially in the context of CaLD families.

Change and sustainability among CaLD family life in the West require an embrace of cultural dynamism and balance.

We need to celebrate our uniqueness and cultural backgrounds as they are our competitive advantage. We need to make room for changes because culture is complex, dynamic, and multidimensional. Let's accept the reality of the prosperous and peaceful coexistence of multiple cultures within the family unit. It's imperative to lead shared rights, respect, and responsibilities within the family. We can keep the big-picture in focus, always directing our thoughts and actions towards family sustainability.

Mental health is human health

Normalizing and humanizing mental health requires urgent attention and collective contribution of everyone in the CaLD family and migrant population. We must stop the stigma within our communities. Let's talk more about it. Let's make it easier for our children to speak even more about it. Modelling this positive, intentional, and courageous attitude towards mental health would significantly improve our wellbeing and enhance sustainability for CaLD families.

It's time to normalize seeking therapy where necessary and unashamedly. Likewise, we can encourage more members of CaLD communities to undertake training and specialisations in the human services and help industries due to the current growing demand, including human resources and talent management, youth services, nursing, aged care practice, counselling, psychology, medicine, psychiatry, etc.

CaLD people can own and lead their sustainability

The message in this book has provided intending, new, and not-so-new immigrants with the information and motivation to consider all aspects of the immigration value chain that will ensure sustainability for their families. Other stakeholders have enjoyed learning about the lived experiences of culturally diverse families. Hopefully, they are inspired. We are all in this together.

Whatever we do, let's remember to prioritize family. It's worth it!

You may also be interested in the following books by Ephraim Osaghae

A HANDBOOK FOR MIGRANTS

The Good, The Challenges, and The Lessons

Ephraim Osaghae

A Reflective Guide for Meaningful and Whole-Life Experience

A Handbook for Migrants: The Good, The Challenges and The Lessons

A Reflective Guide for Meaningful and Whole-Life Experience

In this book, you will find the following:

- Who really is a migrant?

- The career and business challenges of a migrant; and proposed solutions.

- The challenges and lessons with regards to family life including raising children and youths.

- The essential aspects and preparation for aging and retirement.

- The importance of communities and leadership.

- The lived experiences of a migrant.

You will find great use for the content of this book if you are:

- Intending migrants looking for pre-migration considerations and tips.

- Migrants looking for guidance in work, families, youths, and community engagements.

- Non-migrants, students, policymakers, service providers and community leaders.

This book also allows you to participate in meaningful conversations on migrant experiences.

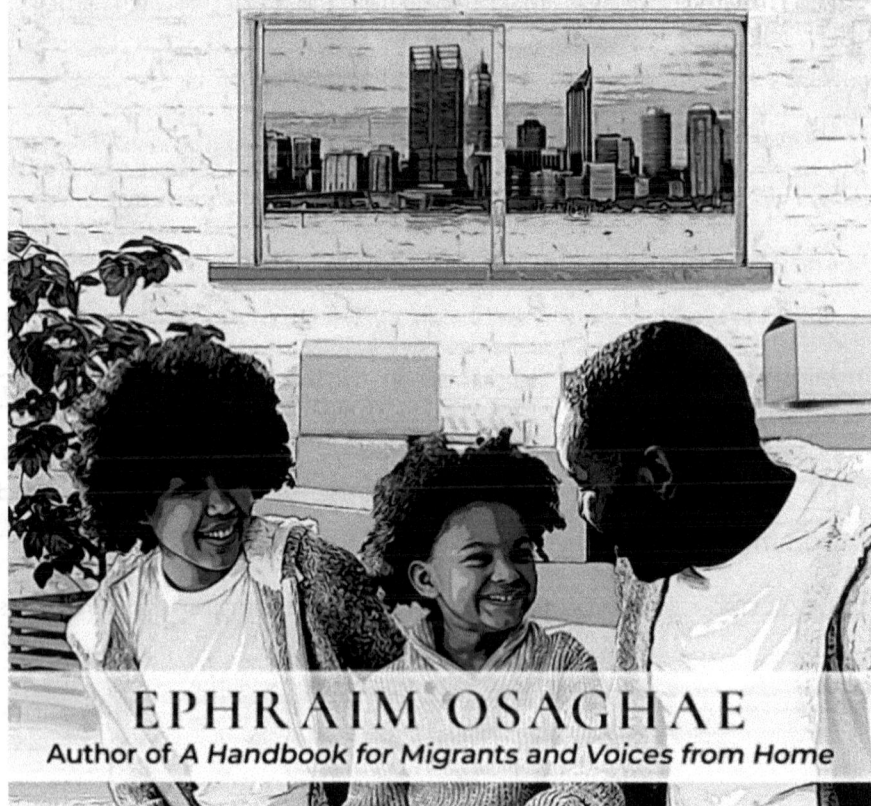

ADOPT
An Amazing Triple A Guide
ADAPT
For Successful Relocation
ACHIEVE
Change and Integration

EPHRAIM OSAGHAE
Author of *A Handbook for Migrants and Voices from Home*

Adopt Adapt Achieve

An Amazing Triple A Guide for Successful Relocation,
Change and Integration

Written for all ages and cultural backgrounds, this extraordinary story takes about an hour to read, but the insights can last a lifetime, with knowledge you can hand down to future generations.

This book reveals hard and unknown truths about relocation, change and integration. And focuses on crucial tactics to **Adopt** and **Adapt** to **Achieve** your goals for the big move.

The author of the book writes from two decades of personal experiences and research in relocating from Africa to Australia - the many successes to enjoy, the pitfalls to avoid, and principles for guidance. The narrative includes snippets from his in-depth interactions with diverse members of the community including immigrants, students, professionals, locals, service providers, workers, business people, government officials, and policymakers.

When you know the real stories of real people, you can prepare yourself better on how to deal with change. You can be careful not to repeat mistakes and go on with less stress and more success in your journey even as you consider your family, career, and healthy ageing.

Non-immigrants will find useful hints and tips in reading this book given the increasing need for cultural integration in our schools, workplaces, neighbourhoods, and communities.

VOICES FROM
Home

WISDOM FROM OUR DIASPORIC ROOTS

EPHRAIM OSAGHAE MBL

Voices from Home: Wisdom from Our Diasporic Roots

A Narration of Parents of First-Generation Migrants

Every human being is part of a bigger family, which is figuratively represented by the *family tree*. We have roots that extend beyond places and cultures of our current residences. Our roots still weigh a lot into our everyday living irrespective of geographical distance and time.

- This book will provide inspiration, some incentives, and a compass for teachable minds to explore and tap into the wealth of their roots.

- It provides insights on the key dynamics and interplay of cultures, underpinning motivations, and extended family structures of typical first-generation migrants.

- It informs global audiences about lived experiences of people of migrant backgrounds starting with the Australian context.

- It contributes to the value-adding conversations around the themes of identity, cross-cultural intelligence, sustainable migration, etc.

- It provides hints and tips for relevant policy makers, service providers, and other government officials, especially in the areas of sustainable migration.

HOW TO ACHIEVE
SUCCESSFUL
MIGRATION AND
INTEGRATION

Turning what could have been threats and
weaknesses to opportunities and strengths

WORKBOOK

EPHRAIM OSAGHAE MBL, PMP, MBA

How to Achieve Successful Migration and Integration (Workbook)

Turning what could have been threats and weaknesses to opportunities and strengths

The focus of this workbook is to provide practical information and wisdom for getting the best value out of the investments in the big move of migration, relocation, and integration.

The key aspects of migration value chain are covered in the book including factors to consider as part of pre-migration preparations, setting SMART goals, and settling well into your new location.

Learn:

- How to prepare prior to your relocation

- How to transition and settle well in the new location

- How to adopt, adapt and be successful in achieving your goals

- How to sustain the achievement of your goals

Readers and users will learn and receive guidance based on real stories of real people that should lead to real actions for success.

A HANDBOOK *for* MIGRANT YOUTH

PEER TO PEER WISDOM FROM THOSE WHO'VE BEEN THERE, DONE THAT

LiME Youth

Compiled by Ephraim Osaghae

A Handbook for Migrant Youth

Peer To Peer Wisdom From Those Who've Been There,
Done That

A Glimpse into the World of Migrant Youth. A vibrant group of multicultural youth group presents what it takes to make it as a young migrant - to live to the fullest, to achieve your dreams and to enjoy the experience. Prepare yourself for insights, stories and lessons from their lives, and the acumen they have gathered from the LiME Project.

All young people, migrants as well as those who are already established in the new country will find information in this book very useful. And they can use it to inspire others as well.

Parents, mentors, teachers, and school administrators will find valuable tips and suggestions in this book that will help them in their ongoing efforts to make great leaders of their children, mentees, and students.

The content in this book will also provide government office holders, policy makers and service providers with real stories and lived experiences from young people themselves.

Finally, while Australia is the context for this book, the principles and lessons are applicable across the globe.

TOP
INSIDERS GUIDE
—— FOR ——
SUCCESSFUL
—— AND ——
STABLE CAREERS

How to Secure and Sustain Professional Jobs
Without Losing Self and Value

EPHRAIM OSAGHAE
MBA, MBL, PMP

Top Insiders Guide To Successful And Stable Careers

How to Secure and Sustain Professional Jobs Without Losing Self and Value

From two decades of lived experiences (as a skilled immigrant himself, residential professional, and expat work in Africa, Australia, The Middle East, Europe, USA, and Asia, and his extensive NGO work), Ephraim Osaghae addresses tough questions about navigating your new country for successful and stable careers.

He believes that when you learn from real stories of real people and selfless insiders, you can prepare yourself better on how to deal with change, relocation, and other major shifts in life. You can take the necessary actions to maximize gains, minimize pains, and achieve your goals.

This quick and easy-to-read guide book:

- Unpacks the foundational principles of maximizing your strengths, managing your weaknesses, and achieving your goals.

- Reveals master frameworks for communication, qualifications, work experience, and networking.

- Teaches you to understand the critical place of showing up!

While intending, new and relatively more settled immigrants are the ideal audience for this book, non-immigrants and other stakeholders will also find useful hints and tips for job-seeking and cultural intelligence.

MIGRAPRENEURS

The Potentials for Diversifying Our Diversity

EPHRAIM OSAGHAE

MBA, MBL, PMP

Migrapreneurs

The Potentials for Diversifying our Diversity

Immigrants are people who have moved to new countries in order to settle as permanent residents or naturalized citizens. This valuable resource is primarily for them; especially those having doubts about their potentials and entrepreneurial skills, and applying the advantages in their new locations.

Give a man (or a woman) a fish and you feed him for a day;

Teach a man (or a woman) to fish and you feed him for a lifetime;

What about the man or woman owning a pond or two containing fishes?

This book provides exclusive insights into *Migrapreneurs* (migrants + entrepreneurship), the *who, what, why,* and *how.* It will inform, inspire, and challenge readers to courageously exploit the advantages of their diversity in the context of entrepreneurship and business. They can take charge of their destinies by creating robust options while depending less on the already challenged economic and social welfare systems in the new countries.

Before you start reading, please prepare your mind for a journey that requires discipline and focus. What this book offers you is a path most immigrants don't take due to *can't-do* mindset, scarcity mentality, fear of the unknown, and lack of appropriate support. Reading this book, and taking prescribed actions, will assuredly provide you with a trigger for getting on the path to greatness.

www.ingramcontent.com/pod-product-compliance
Lightning Source LLC
Chambersburg PA
CBHW062144020426
42334CB00020B/2499